10665757

Alliance Politics

ISBN 0-231-03066-5 *Cloth*

ISBN 0-231-08307-6 *Paperback*

COPYRIGHT © 1970 RICHARD E. NEUSTADT

ISBN: 0 231 03066 5

LIBRARY OF CONGRESS CATALOG CARD NUMBER: 77-120855

PRINTED IN THE UNITED STATES OF AMERICA

9 8 7 6 5 4 3 2

RICHARD E. NEUSTADT

Alliance Politics

COLUMBIA UNIVERSITY PRESS

New York and London

The Radner Lectures

IN 1956 THE Radner Family Foundation established a
lectureship at Columbia University in memory of Wil-
liam Radner, a graduate of Columbia College and The
Columbia Law School. Since his career in the public
service had been terminated by his untimely death, the
gift appropriately stipulated that these lectures were to
deal with subjects in the field of public law and government. Previous Radner Lectures were:

1959 Harry S Truman, Former President of the United
States
"The Presidency"

1960 Lord Boothby, Rector of the University of St. Andrew's
"Parliament and the Profession of Politics in Britain"

1963 Robert R. Bowie, Director of the Center for Interna-
tional Affairs, and Dillon Professor of International
Relations, Harvard University
"Present and Future in Foreign Policy"

1965 Lord Harlech, Former British Ambassador to the
United States
"Must the West Decline?"

For BERT, BETH, and DICK

Preface

IN 1965 I HAD occasion to testify before the Jackson Subcommittee of the United States Senate. Its hearings at that time were on the state of North Atlantic Treaty institutions, a subject other witnesses had taken very seriously. Their seriousness left me skeptical. I tried to put my skepticism into words:

Alliance institutions, civil and military, are not sovereign states—though SHAPE at one time often played the part and got away with it—but rather they are creatures, or at least creations, of the governments concerned. Thus their importance turns on their symbolic quality, together with their actual capacity (which often is not very great) to influence the work of men inside those governments.

Because allies are governments, each is a more or less complex arena for internal bargaining among the bureaucratic elements and political personalities who collectively comprise its working apparatus. Its action is the product of their interaction. They bargain not at random but according to the processes, conforming to the perquisites, responsive to the pressures of their own political system.

It follows that relationships between allies are something like relationships between two great American departments. These are relationships of vast machines with different histories, routines, preoccupations, prospects. Each machine is worked by men with different personalities, skills, drives, responsibilities. Each set of men, quite naturally, would rather do his work in independence of the other set. If one government would influence the actions of another, it must find means to convince enough men and the right men on the other side that what it wants is what they need for their own purposes, in their own jobs, comporting with their own internally inspired hopes and fears, so that they will pursue it for themselves in their own bargaining arena.[1]

Since then I have been thinking of these words. I took them as a theme to ponder and elaborate before an academic audience in 1966, when Columbia University invited me to give the Radner Lectures. What follows is a reworked version of those lectures; here is where reflection on that theme has led me up to now.

While lecturing, it was my hope to light some fires under inquiry in international relations, in comparative government, and in the politics internal to a national machine, especially our own. While writing, I have held to the same hope. This book is meant to open issues, to stir argument, to spur research in spheres far wider than its self-selected limits. I deal here only with two governments, American and British, in two crises, Suez and Skybolt. Even within these limits I would not claim for a moment to have offered the "last word." My lectures were intended to start many things and claimed to finish none. So the case remains.

It is unusual, I know, for three years to elapse between the giving of such lectures and their written presentation; especially when what is written represents a marked elaboration of what had been spoken. For this I plead a combination of too many time constraints with too much curiosity.

What piqued my curiosity was the Suez affair of 1956. In 1966 I knew far less about it than I have discovered since. I still know less than I would like. I have not yet been accorded opportunity to go through certain files of John Foster Dulles at Princeton, or to search the White House MEMCON files at Abilene. At this stage I am still dependent on the minds and notes of friends who either were participants or have had access to those files. My situation on the British side is comparable, though eased by the report that there are no equivalent files (Eden, it is said, had them burned).

Lest Suez research turn into a lifework, I have now decided that for present purposes perhaps I know enough. Readers should understand, however, that what they encounter here regarding these events is my best current judgment, not the definitive word that an historian might offer later.

So now, to the relief of those who sponsor Radner Lectures, I take hands off this manuscript and let it come before you. As I do so I am grateful to my former colleagues at Columbia for giving me the spur of opportunity, and to the Columbia University Press for unexampled patience. I owe gratitude as well to the late President Kennedy, who asked me to research the Skybolt crisis for him, an assignment that set off this train of thought.

Other acknowledgments are in order. I am grateful to the Twentieth Century Fund, which financed a preliminary probe of British sources on Suez, and to the Rockefeller Foundation for twice according me a refuge in that marvelous place to think and write, the Villa Serbelloni. A debt is owed to many friends in Washington and London, witnesses to the events I shall describe, or "in-house" students of them, who let me pick their brains and asked only for anonymity. Another debt is owed the Trustees of the Dulles Papers in the Princeton Library, who gave me access to a part of their collection, notably the Secretary's annotated calendars.

Still another debt, a heavy one, is owed the members of the Senior Common Room of Nuffield College, who introduced me, a decade ago, to the intriguing mysteries of British government and who have given me since then a base for work in England, a source of informed counsel, and the warmth of lasting friendships.

Finally, I am grateful to my present Harvard colleagues at the Kennedy School and its Institute of Politics, especially to members of our Research Seminar on Bureaucracy, Politics, and Policy, a venture I shall tell you more about in Chapter VI. They listened, read and hand-held while this work was being done. Among them let me single out my colleague Graham Allison, who helped at every stage. In the last stage of this project I had help as well from Suzanne Weaver, who lived up to her rightful reputation for first-rate research assistance. And Pennie Gouzoule, helpful as always, matched patience with perseverance in deciphering my awful scrawl. Results of course are my responsibility, not theirs.

RICHARD E. NEUSTADT

Cambridge, Massachusetts
December, 1969

Contents

Alliance Politics

I: *Allies at Odds*

DURING the twelve years between the close of the Korean War in 1953 and Americanization of the Vietnam War in 1965, the United States twice found itself in public controversy of the sharpest sort with its most intimate peacetime ally, the United Kingdom. In each case, controversy swelled into a crisis of confidence, a suspension of intimacy, almost breaking relations in one instance, straining them hard in the other.

The first and more severe of these two Anglo-American crises came in 1956 after nationalization of the Suez Canal, when Britain, France, and Israel resorted to force against Egypt. The second of these crises came in 1962 with American cancellation of "Skybolt," an air-to-surface missile which the British needed to sustain their claim of independence as a nuclear power.

My purpose here is to explore those crises in some depth for what they can suggest about relationships between two governments, one of them ours, when each has been habituated to regard the other as a peacetime "friend." For in the years ahead, as in the past decades, it is to be presumed that Washington will deal with many other governments allied to us for peacetime undertakings, habitually viewed as well disposed to us, whose acquiescence or support we claim for our own causes, as

they claim ours for theirs. It thus is timely to consider
what may be the nature of such friendly relations: the
hazards in them, the conditions for their maintenance.
Since we apparently cannot escape peacetime alliances,
we would do well to understand as best we can their uses
and limitations, how they work, and where they tend to
fail.

Alliance politics, by which I mean relations of this
sort, is but one aspect of a vastly wider subject, international relations, and invokes problems of inquiry associated with the whole realm of comparative government.
Peacetime relations are not altogether unlike those of
wartime. Relations of alliance are not altogether different from relations of indifference, or of enmity. Internal
politics affects external ties and thus must be accounted
for in studying those ties, not only when the Anglo-
Saxons come together but whenever any government relates to any other. Everything discovered in an explora-
tion of two crises between two allies has implications for
these wider fields. Indeed, it is a secondary purpose here
to hoist these implications into view, so you can ponder
them. But I shall not address them. That I leave to you.
I am intent upon a narrower concern: American relations with our own peacetime allies.

In short, I now propose a close look at the task of in-
fluencing such allies toward courses of action we ap-
prove: looking at that task as it presents itself to those
who have to do it, men inside the government of the
United States.

Suez and Skybolt are cases in point. As a prelude to
analysis, the next two chapters summarize these cases

chronologically, each in turn. Thereafter I shall draw upon them interchangeably, without heeding chronology, for purposes of illustration. The summaries, I hope, will make ensuing illustrations easy to follow.

Before we turn to cases, it is well to note their biases. Then I am not misleading you, nor you misreading me.

In the first place, what I offer here are negative examples. These are cases of conflict, of cross-purposes, of breakdown followed by emergency repairs, costly for all concerned. I choose these not because I think them typical, far from it. I choose them rather because crises tend at once to be illuminating and remembered. Failure is a lightning flash, exposing salient features: participants recall it, journalists review it, historians record it, and contemporaries carry it in context. For most of you these crises are contemporaneous. That is not the least of their utility to me. It saves a lot of words.

Secondly, the Anglo-American relationship—in Whitehall terminology, "the special relationship"—is itself a source of bias to the extent that it actually is "special." In the time span of these crises, the connections between Washington and London ran both wide and deep. Not only formal pledges but long-standing institutional arrangements joined these governments at many levels, mixing them up with one another in all sorts of working ways, mostly as the heritage of World War II. History and language and acquaintance added qualitative strength to those entanglements. So did a sense of shared external interests, global in scope. Beneath all these, supporting all, were the foundations of felt need. Emphatically, in 1956, and only a little less so six years later, we conceived we needed Britain in our business, for our purposes, while Whitehall took the obverse as a matter of course.

Leaving aside client-states, protectorates, and dependencies, it can be said that these two governments, the British and American, never had external ties so variegated and so tight—and so sustained—as those to one another in the generation after World War II. Indeed, throughout the modern history of peacetime friendships among major powers there is nothing comparable, save the Austro-German linkage in the generation before World War I. The Entente-Cordiale is not in the same class, as Charles de Gaulle could tell you—and as we shall see.

Accordingly, the pattern of behavior found in Suez and in Skybolt need be treated with appropriate reserve. What these two crises suggest about the dealings between governments may not suffice to characterize Washington's relations with a capital less intimate than London a few years ago, not even London in another span of time. Presumably, such dealings change their character in some degree along a spectrum of habitual relations running from intimacy toward hostility. Washington and Paris, I presume, would not now interact precisely as did Washington and London. If so, we deal here with but one end of the spectrum. I await research by others to decide in what degree a move along it makes a difference in behavior.

It would be wrong, however, to assume that London's links to Washington in 1956 or 1962 were *altogether* different from the links of other governments with comparable status and accustomed claims on friendship. No

more than in the case of others was this ever a true "partnership of equals." The inequality, quite naturally, has
deepened over time: more marked after Suez than before, more marked in the Sixties than the Fifties, more
marked now than in the early Sixties. But even in the
middle Fifties, London, though more trusted and in
some respects more stable, was about as central to the
hopes and fears of Washington as Bonn today, or Tokyo
perhaps a few years hence: a "middle power," neither
equal nor vassal, which history, geography, or economics
rendered specially significant to us for the time being.

Britain was but the first such middle power to emerge
after World War II, leveling down from ruinous victory
while others leveled up from ruinous defeat. We now
count several in the Northern Hemisphere; others are
perhaps emergent to the south. Some or all will figure
largely in our own concerns as far ahead as I can see. Our
two crises of confidence with Britain punctuate a friendship which, despite its special features, bears an interesting resemblance to all friendships of the sort. Among
other things, Suez and Skybolt tell us much about divergences in power between friends—at least so long as
one of them is Washington.

Thirdly, to apply a two-power perspective to these
crises is to simplify friendly relations. This substitutes an
artificial world for the real world. Reality is not bilateral.
Conflicts between governments such as Washington and
London scarcely could arise on matters of concern to
them alone. Nor did they in these cases. In the Suez
crisis, France, and later Israel, were London's partners,
objects of American concern throughout, while Egypt
set the stage, Russia played the "heavy," and the United

Nations furnished a Greek chorus. In the Skybolt case, while Paris was not actually a party to this conflict, the dispute diverted Washington and London from contemporary dealings with the French on matters more important to them both than was the substance of their quarrel with one another. Conceivably, these crises made more impact, left more traces, in Paris than in London or in Washington. The policy and postures of de Gaulle owed much, it seems, to lessons drawn from Suez and to opportunities afforded after Skybolt.

If one seeks an enlargement of the present frame of reference, encompassing more governments than two, these crises will serve nicely for the purpose. I leave that task, however, to the specialists on France, Egypt, or Israel. America and England are as much as I can manage. They suffice to make a start.

Finally, the evidence I offer suffers all the failings of historical reconstruction, compounded by security and sensitivity. On both sides of the Atlantic, Suez and Skybolt were bruising affairs, within the two governments as well as between them. Egos were involved—and reputations. Much of what occurred was not recorded; everything recorded was classified. The recollections of participants remain available, but memory lapses are compounded by discretion. And John Foster Dulles is dead; while Harold Macmillan, although very much alive, assiduously avoids scooping his own memoirs.

Happily, the press was much engaged on both occasions; leaks abounded. This is some compensation. For Suez there is further compensation in the outpouring of articles and books by which participants and journalists feed English fascination with the last gasp of Empire.[2]

For Skybolt I myself have compensation in the happen-
stance that I researched both sides of the affair, soon after
the event, as part of a consulting assignment from the
late President Kennedy. This is a help to me but not to
you, since I am not at liberty to do more than elaborate
what already is in the public record. Fortunately for
us both, knowledgeable journalists and former White
House aides have put a lot on record.[3]

Incidentally, let me note for you to ponder one conclusion from my privileged view of Skybolt. In Washington, at least, the telephone and copying machine
combine to falsify the files as sources of historical reconstruction. The one may leave no record, while the other
makes so many that few men entrust their own full
thoughts to paper. In London, up to now, these inven-
tions have had less impact, but similar results may be
produced by the convention of the "Ministerial Secret."
Were a student made to choose, God forbid, between the
files and memories of participants, he would do well to
take the latter. Pity the future historian, who may turn
out worse off than those of us who have to work with relatively journalistic means.

At any rate, the reconstructions I can offer here are
but approximations. Like all such, these are built of
bits and pieces drawn from published works and private interviews, laced heavily with inferences drawn from
judgment. It is my judgment. I am stuck with it. You
may take it or not as you choose.

So much for biases. Now we can turn to those cases.

II: The Suez Crisis

IN TIME and in significance the Suez case comes first. As a crisis in Anglo-American relations it occupied the final months of 1956. But roots run back to earlier events. This case cannot be understood in terms of 1956 alone. There is a sort of tragic hero here, Anthony Eden. To see his stakes in 1956 we need to note his stance in 1954.

I

During the summer of 1954 the British Government, Winston Churchill's Conservative ministry, reluctantly acceded to a further alteration of its dispositions in the Middle East, pegged on the proposition that accord with the new government of Egypt could be parlayed into Western-oriented, stabilized relations for the region. Having previously yielded its political protectorate and military occupation of the country, London now negotiated with the President of Egypt, Gamal Abdel Nasser, a withdrawal from the British base commanding the Suez Canal, effective July, 1956. The Canal itself was to continue until 1969 as the concession of a private French concern in which the British government held a controlling interest. But for the first time since the 1880s,

British forces would be gone from the canal and altogether out of Egypt.

The man who argued this arrangement through the Tory Cabinet despite majority reluctance there, and Churchill's own distaste, and outrage on right-wing back benches, was the then Foreign Secretary, Anthony Eden, whose diplomatic mastery was generally acknowledged. So was his place as Churchill's heir-apparent. Although this proved the most divisive issue in the second Churchill government, and although it left scars—among them a strong, organized back-bench minority, the "Suez Group" —Eden gained the acquiescence of his colleagues. Their decision, incidentally, much pleased Washington, which had been pressing for it. This, no doubt, was part of Eden's argument.

Nine months later, in the spring of 1955, Churchill resigned. Eden succeeded and then went to the country on the theme of "peace." He also sent to Washington for help in that endeavor, and he got it from his old wartime collaborator, the American President, Dwight David Eisenhower. Despite the President's dubiety and the extreme reluctance of his Secretary of State, John Foster Dulles, Eisenhower joined Eden in arranging a Geneva "Summit Conference" with the Russians for July. Not accidentally, this was announced before the British General Election, which the Tories won handily.

The Summit Conference then ensued and left an afterglow, the "Spirit of Geneva" as the British and American press put it. This was punctured in September by announcement of an arms deal between Cairo and Prague (in those days tantamount to Moscow). That Nasser had been looking for more arms than we would give him was well known in Washington and London through the summer. But the notion that the Soviets would give him some—thus entering the Middle Eastern scene in direct fashion—had been discounted so heavily that nothing had been said to them about it at the Summit. When it happened, Washington and London were embarrassed. They also were disturbed about unsettling effects upon the Arab-Jewish balance in the unresolved dispute set off by Israel's independence. Along with France, they had been pledged since 1950 in a Tripartite Declaration to defend whichever side became the victim of aggression from the other. They and the French had doled out arms to both sides with a careful eye for balance, holding back on weapons of offense. Now their monopoly of arms supply was broken.

But by the time this happened Eisenhower was in an oxygen tent, the victim of a heart attack which followed six weeks after he had led his delegation at the Summit. The American government, accordingly, stood almost still. Not until December were we able, with the British, to decide upon an interim response to Soviet support for Egypt. This took the form of opening up prospects for far more material American support of Egypt in another sphere, economic development: we offered tentatively to join Britain and the World Bank in a three-way undertaking to build Nasser's favorite project for development, a high dam at Aswan on the Nile. Dulles, although doubtful of the venture, took the lead in pressing the World Bank to work it out so Nasser might see reason to turn westward again.

This approach was not long lived. Within six months

the British and Americans were both on the point of abandoning it, and with it short-term efforts to conciliate Nasser. Their growing coolness stemmed in part from problems with the project. Underlying these was disenchantment with appeasement in the longer aftermath of Nasser's arms deal. As the months passed, he showed no signs of reviewing or undoing his new-found relations with the East. Quite the contrary.[4]

By July 1956, London was advising Washington to let the Aswan project fade away. For a variety of reasons, especially congressional resentment against Nasser, Dulles decided to do so. Eisenhower approved. But they did not "play it long" as London had expected. Instead, to head off Senate action barring any aid for Egypt, Dulles saw Nasser's envoy on July 19 and calmly withdrew us from the project. This was tantamount to calling it off.[5]

II

One week later, on July 26, Nasser nationalized the Suez Canal. (The last British troops had left their base two weeks before.) Nasser gave as his reason American abandonment of Aswan and his need for compensating funds from Canal revenues. That reason may or may not have been real. It fixed, however, on our Secretary of State a public role at home—and in London—as precipitating agent of the crisis.

Neither Washington nor London had anticipated this particular event. Instead both had expected possible appeals for help from Cairo to Moscow. By now, apparently, Eden and Eisenhower alike, along with Dulles, were reconciled to that: Nasser deserved the Russians; let him stew in their juice and see where it got him. When he did otherwise—perhaps in deference to our dislike for his arms deal—Washington and London were surprised. On our side surprise was mixed with chagrin. In London there was also outrage; its dimensions soon became our chief concern.

The British were seized by a spasm of anger, none more than the Prime Minister. For them, as for all Western Europe, the Canal was an essential artery of trade. Among other things, a great part of their oil imports came through it. To many sober citizens—Cabinet Ministers, men in the street, leader-writers of the London *Times*—"Egyptian" spelled "incompetent": ships would run aground, the banks would cave, the bottom would silt up. For Englishmen, moreover, and especially for Tories, the Canal had connotations apart from commerce. It was vividly symbolic: Empire, Victoria, Disraeli. Nasser, furthermore, was violating treaties in the manner of the dictators of twenty years before. The parallel seemed striking: every Minister had memories; none more so than Stanley Baldwin's Foreign Secretary, now Prime Minister.

Within a week the Cabinet, Eden in the van, had privately decided to restore Western control of the Canal by force, unless negotiation would suffice to do it, in the process squelching Nasser once and for all: invasion would serve to unseat him. That resolve, though unannounced because contingent, seemed to square with current sentiment in the House of Commons and the country.

The President got wind of this at once in private messages from Eden and also from his other wartime friend,

Harold Macmillan, now Chancellor of the Exchequer. Eisenhower evidently was appalled. For us the Canal was neither life line nor symbol, nor was Nasser public enemy number one. The President of the United States would soon campaign for re-election in November on the twin themes of "prosperity" and "peace." He sought the largest possible majority, in hopes of dragging by his coattails enough Congressmen and Senators to restore his party's control of both Houses of Congress, lost two years before. Eisenhower had been induced to run despite ill health by pleas from his associates, Dulles included, that his country needed him to keep the peace (and a Republican majority in Congress to support him). Nothing suggests that they or he were cynics.

Besides, symbols of other people's empires had negative connotations, especially English symbols—reminiscent of George III—the more so since our Communist competitors played "anti-imperialist" to the third world. Nasser posed a problem, presently unpleasant and potentially unbearable; but use of force to solve it—especially the force of Egypt's former master—would not do, save in a "last resort" dictated by an obvious necessity. Nationalization of a property in Egypt thirteen years before the end of its concession did not count. Necessity awaited palpable mismanagement of the Canal, or other provocation, palpably adverse to the Community of Nations. So Eisenhower was to state, perhaps over-politely, in subsequent letters to Eden.[6]

At the start of August, Eisenhower sent Dulles to London. By all accounts, he went there under orders both to help the British and to keep the peace. Two weeks later, a first London Conference of twenty-two maritime powers met on Eden's invitation and addressed the issue of restoring Canal management, ownership aside, to status independent of a single nation's politics. The invitation was Eden's, but the concept of a conference on that issue had been Dulles's and he took leadership in shaping its outcome. This was a scheme sponsored by eighteen of the conferees—Moscow and Delhi dissenting with two others—for a new international agency, a Suez Canal Board, to run the Canal on Egypt's behalf under United Nations auspices. In the first week of September, a committee of eighteen put that proposition before Nasser. To nobody's surprise he turned it down: Egypt itself would run the Canal on the world's behalf, as impartially as the old company had done or any new board could. Cairo's formal statement was released September 9.[7]

In the eyes of British activists the August gambit had been helpful: Dulles had earned his keep. The conference and its issue and outcome drew a line which now set "eighteen powers," the United States included, against Egypt on an issue of international rights, never mind nationalization. Besides, in August there was nothing else the British could have done. In late July, concerting with the French, they had begun to ready an invasion. But their military staffs insisted on a month of preparation. Dulles had helped them put that interval to use.

The French were partners in the military planning, eager partners, indeed champing at the bit. The government of Guy Mollet, six months in office, had convinced itself of two things: first, that its survival, and indeed that of the Fourth Republic, turned on forceable repression of rebellion in Algeria; second, that the rebels were

dependent on Nasser's support. History would prove
Mollet right on the one score, wrong on the other, but
he did not know this yet. Nasser, therefore, had to be
cut down. Here was a providential opportunity. The
French were of no mind to let it pass. For them there
was only one problem: they were ill-equipped to go it
alone. British transports, carriers, and bases lured them
irresistably into collaboration. This was a "mistake"
French governments have not made since.

While awaiting word from Nasser, London and Paris
polished contingency plans: they would appeal his expected negative to the Security Council of the United
Nations; a Soviet veto on Egypt's behalf could be anticipated. Meanwhile, the old Suez Canal Company, deprived of a "legitimate" successor, would withdraw all
non-Egyptian pilots, three-fourths of the lot, from the
Canal. Chaos would ensue there. Traffic would snarl to
a stop. Anglo-French armed forces then would land and
take possession, incidentally knocking out Egyptian air
power and threatening Cairo with a foreign occupation.
Nasser, thus discredited, would fall; the eighteen-power
scheme would be enforced on his successor. So they
planned. "Musketeer," their military operation, had the
feature that it was to start ten days before the landing
(with Southampton as an embarkation port), testimony
to British unreadiness for limited war at long distance.
Accordingly, a sailing had to follow very quickly on a
"no" from Nasser and a turn to the UN. Otherwise, there
would be an extraordinary pause between a Soviet veto
and an allied landing.

On September 6, the British Cabinet decided to call
Parliament from summer recess for September 12. By

then there would be word from Nasser: Eden could announce both his appeal to the UN and the contingency of force. Having announced the one, Musketeer's lead-time would take him to the other in a matter of days.

III

In the first week of September 1956, Dulles again faced the task he had been set a month before: befriending the British without breaching the peace. Thereupon he improvised a scheme which became known as "SCUA" (Suez Canal Users Association). This would be an agency of maritime powers, initially the eighteen of the London Conference, formed independently of Egypt to take over pilotage through the Canal, receiving in return the tolls of users. Its pilots would be based at sea, its tolls banked abroad. If Egypt acquiesced, she would be out of funds for Canal maintenance, with no recourse but to let SCUA take it over, producing in effect, although not in form, the eighteen-power program. Nonacquiescence would mean blocking the Canal, or sinking SCUA base ships, palpably aggressive acts against a host of nations.

By the time the British Cabinet met September 6 to summon Parliament, Dulles had roughed out this scheme, discussed it with the President, and was engaged in polishing it up. Six days after that, September 12, Eden would rise in Commons. On September 8, Eisenhower dispatched to Eden a long letter conveying strong if generalized distaste for use of force. A day later, on September 9, Nasser spoke his piece. On the evening of September 10, while Mollet was with Eden, fixing the details and date of Musketeer, London received cables on the

SCUA scheme from Dulles. British sources say that on the next day Dulles followed up by telephone in calls to Eden and his Foreign Secretary, Selwyn Lloyd.

With Parliament in session on the morrow, Dulles evidently argued hard: by all accounts he urged against resort to the UN; he urged a trial of SCUA first; he pleaded the advantage of a later turn to New York, if need be, for redress of such grievances as SCUA could produce. But Eden may have heard—or strained to hear—that the United States would be no less aggrieved than Britain. At any rate, it was implicit in the scheme that SCUA's members all must be aggrieved alike. Eden evidently thought these came to the same thing. If so, here was a chance of binding Washington to London and Paris. All he had to trade was time, deferring the UN and Musketeer.

Eden also was aware, no doubt—and so was Dulles—that time already had dulled English appetite for force and cooled down some Tories, while awakening opposition in the ranks of Labour. Also, British military staffs were unenthused, while in the Foreign Office two traditions of great power—the American alignment and pro-Arabism—had combined to chill the bulk of his official advisers. Dulles evidently saw these as constraints which time could strengthen; Eden evidently saw them all dissolved upon a showing of American support which time could buy. Momentarily, these visions overlapped; Eden agreed to give SCUA a try.

This meant that Eden had to make SCUA his own, espousing it in Cabinet and expounding it to Commons, where it would be publicly unveiled for the first time. He, not Dulles, had to take responsibility for advocating what he privately is said to have regarded as a "cockeyed" scheme. This was no mean sacrifice for a Prime Minister to offer the American alliance. It grew the greater when the activists in Cabinet—to say nothing of the French—demurred at delay, and greater still when the ensuing House debate became a shouting match between Nasser-haters and UN-lovers, with Eden perforce in the middle. His sacrifice grew greatest on the second day of that debate with word from Washington that Dulles, at a press conference, had said SCUA should boycott the Canal, not force it, if Egyptians chose to block it: ". . . we don't intend to go into that shooting . . . . we intend to send our boats round the Cape."

Eden had been suffering since spring from a recurrent fever and from bouts of extreme nervous irritation caused by faulty surgery: a badly patched bile duct. Dulles's performance, in the midst of his own, rubbed ragged nerves. Reportedly, Eden was furious; as even his memoirs record, he conceived himself double-crossed. Still, diverting boats, a boycott, was not without promise: Nasser would be hurt and the Americans would be in step, with dollars to pay extra costs. Besides, Eden was committed: SCUA now was his. On reflection he evidently cooled down. His people soon were starting to elaborate measures of economic coercion.

On September 19 there occurred a second London Conference, Dulles in attendance once again, to seek agreement of potential member governments on SCUA's scope and form. By then, however, Egypt had been running the Canal successfully for three days in the absence of company pilots. These had departed according to plan. Now Egyptian nationals and others, hired from every-

where, were piloting ships safely. On the first day, forty
vessels made the transit; in a week, 254. What was the
case for coercion? To say nothing of pilots and tolls. In
British eyes the answer remained boycott to enforce justice: the international rights defined at the first London
Conference. Aside from the French, however, there were
almost no takers for that answer at this second Conference. And the taker who mattered, Dulles, evaded with
the rest: Washington could neither commit private shippers to diversion in advance of trouble nor promise in
advance to pay the extra dollar costs of tanker-time
around the Cape and oil from Venezuela. Dulles did his
best to keep the Conference from collapsing and achieved
agreement for a further session in October which would
formally bring SCUA into being. For British activists
and their French friends, this was cold comfort.

Dulles flew to Washington September 21. While he
was in the air, London and Paris announced that they
would take their grievances to the UN Security Council.
He had been with Eden just before departure but had
heard nothing of this. Now, by all accounts, it was
Dulles who felt double-crossed.

With evident American approval the Security Council
took its time. The Anglo-French complaint was scheduled for October 5. Dulles did his best to see that once
the issue went there, contrary to his advice, it would be
handled in low key: a stage in negotiation, not a prelude
to force. In this he was of one mind with Dag Hammarskjold, the UN Secretary General, who had strong
support from Delhi, Nasser's friend throughout the crisis,
and from Cairo. Nasser treated these proceedings with
the same restraint and care he had accorded manage-

ment of the Canal. At American urging, London and Paris moderated their tone and softened their demands. At Hammarskjold's urging, their foreign ministers met privately with him and Nasser's envoy to secure a basis for direct negotiations. The upshot was a British statement of "six principles," accepted by all sides. Although the Soviets vetoed a formal resolution to effect these through the medium of SCUA, the Egyptians promised to consider other means informally presented them by Hammarskjold. Cairo agreed also to resume the private meetings in Geneva at the end of the month.

The issue now was down to whether SCUA, or some counterpart, could intervene in Canal management on its own say-so, or whether it should merely be advisory, appealing differences with Egypt's managers to the UN or the World Court. The French and British argued for the first; the Soviets with Egypt for the second. Behind this issue lay a concrete problem: right of passage for Israeli vessels, which the UN once had ordered but never implemented. Behind this issue, also, lay the question facing French and British activists: was Nasser to escape "scot-free"? They scarcely could make war on such an issue, and they knew it.

So did Washington. The night before the Security Council vote, which left the issue to direct negotiation, Eisenhower told a campaign television audience, "it looks like here is a very great crisis . . . behind us." That statement came October 12.

But unbeknownst to Washington, the British Cabinet, nine days earlier, had sanctioned an entirely different issue as occasion for the use of force. On October 3, Eden

gained approval from his colleagues to launch Musketeer
as a "peace-keeping" operation if Israel attacked Egypt.
What he may not have told them, or not all of them, in
full is that Israeli plans were being instigated by the
French, contingent on British support: the issue thus
would be of their own making.

Resentment against Washington spurred Cabinet approval. On October 2 another Dulles press conference
had tuned American ears for the forthcoming UN proceedings. Among other things inimical to British ears, he
had remarked of SCUA, "There is some talk of teeth
being pulled out of the plan, but I know of no teeth;
there were no teeth in it." This for the front benchers
who had gone through House debate two weeks before—
while Eden made his sacrifice on Dulles's behalf! By all
accounts, their anger was unbounded. Nothing could as-
suage it like a fresh excuse for Musketeer, which left
out the Americans. Eden, angriest of all, served that dish
up to them. They ate it, spiced by loyalty to their leader.

They did so with a confidence born of miscalculation.
The Chancellor of the Exchequer, Harold Macmillan,
had just returned from Washington on unrelated business, where he briefly had seen his friend, the President,
and also Dulles. A man of strength and buoyancy in
Cabinet, who had argued from the first for using force,
Macmillan now reportedly expressed himself convinced
that "Ike will lie doggo" until the election.

This reinforced a notion in the back of Eden's mind,
reportedly as great a comfort to him as Macmillan's word,
or greater: Eisenhower surely could not help but draw
a parallel between the two Canals, Suez and Panama.

Americans might need the precedent of Musketeer; this too should keep them quiet.

IV

So we come to the finale of this crisis. In secrecy a diplomatic "cover story" was prepared: Israel would attack Egypt on the Sinai Peninsula, with France and Britain intervening to protect the Canal. Their ultimatum would demand that both belligerents withdraw from its vicinity; Egypt would refuse; they then would occupy the area by force to save world commerce. A military plan, supposedly consistent with this story, was concocted from Franco-Israeli staff work on the Sinai action juxtaposed to Musketeer. It was not a happy combination. On British insistence, Israeli paratroops had to turn up at once in western Sinai, so the Canal could be "threatened." On Israeli insistence, strikes against Egyptian airpower had to take place on the second day of Musketeer so their lines could be secure from air attack. On French insistence, Anglo-French invasion had to come no more than five days after air strikes. But on British insistence it could not come sooner: their military planners held that paratroops would have to be supported within hours by a sea-borne force, and Musketeer's ship schedules had but little flexibility. Warships would sail from Malta, to say nothing of troops from Southampton; after seventy-eight years of British occupation, Cyprus, although handy, lacked deep-water ports. These trade-offs in the military plan proved fatal to the cover story. Nevertheless, both plan and story were launched October 29. The American election remained eight days away.

Between October 3 and 29, Washington naturally was told nothing. Neither were most British ministers below Cabinet rank, nor any senior permanent officials save the Cabinet Secretary and the Undersecretary of the Foreign Office (himself a strong advocate of force). Cabinet members knew, along with military staffs, and that sufficed for governmental action. Washington, however, had alternative sources of various sorts, sufficient to inform it about military plans and concentrations. By late October, it was plain that trouble impended from Israel, in which the French and British were involved. But timing was unknown and Dulles remained tranquil. Apparently he thought we had been told by Lloyd, in private conversation at the UN, that before the British moved we could expect to be consulted.[8] Moreover, Dulles and associates reportedly assumed that at a moment of supreme importance to the West, our allies would restrain impetuous Israelis.

For not only were we nearing our election day, but it was coming on the heels of an upheaval in Eastern Europe, a veritable rending of the Communist bloc, a climactic moment in the course of the Cold War, replete with opportunities and risks. The moment offered an apparent vindication, deeply felt, of a world view expounded by Administration spokesmen, especially Dulles. On October 17 there suddenly ensued a palace revolution in Warsaw, unthroning Stalinists while seizing from the Russians full control over the army and police. This was managed from within the Polish Communist Party and was enforced on Moscow by a threat to raise the nation against Soviet troops. On October 22, even as the Russians were conceding to the Poles, a popular revolt began in Budapest. To contain it there ensued a comparable coup within the Hungarian Party, and the Soviets conceded troop withdrawals from the capital on October 29, the day Israel marched.

At that moment Washington was giving what attention it could spare from our election to events in Hungary, seeking by all means at its disposal to keep world attention riveted upon them without seeming to exploit them for itself—eyes on, hands off—in hopes that Moscow might continue with concessions. From a policy standpoint, this seemed of first importance for the West.

Eisenhower did not question that his nearest allies saw it so. When, despite two pleas from him, Israeli forces crossed the Egyptian border, he publicly invoked both the United Nations and the Tripartite Declaration. He announced that he would now consult with the two other signatories of that Declaration on measures needed to restore the border. Within hours, he was reading on press cables of their ultimatum, not alone to Israel but also to Egypt. He learned thereby that they conceived the Declaration he invoked as a dead letter. He also learned, for it was obvious enough, that Israel had acted as a stalking horse for their resort to force. All this at such a time! By all accounts, his anger was profound: "They did not tell me." The sentiment apparently was shared by his associates, aghast at the lese majesté—not least by Dulles, the man who had been told to keep the peace.

Worse was to come. On October 31, the British bombed Egyptian airfields while Israeli columns raced across Sinai. Then "nothing happened," no invasion followed: the Canal remained in Egypt's hands and ships were sunk to block it. Reportedly, this drove the President wild. It put him on the rack in the last week before election, and it put his wayward allies into an insane position. As allied plans unfolded, he, the general, is said to have been astounded: waywardness was bad enough; incompetence required punishment.

Washington's reactions evidently altered as the week progressed. We seem to have begun by trying to escape all onus, putting on a public face to match the private fact. We ended by administering punishment. At the start, we jockeyed with the Russians to be first with a cease-fire resolution in a hastily called session of the Security Council. The British and French were not yet engaged. We saw this as a substitute for their ultimatum. But they, wanting no substitute, vetoed both resolutions.

Then, mindful of Budapest, we fostered Soviet collaboration in a turn to the General Assembly, under the "Uniting for Peace" procedure of Korean days, which Moscow hitherto had scorned. The Assembly, lacking mandatory powers, could put "world opinion" on the record by a two-thirds vote, not subject to veto. Soviet-American alignment behind Egypt meant the votes. Our allies knew it. Debate was scheduled for November 2. When it came, there still was no invasion. The next day the Assembly voted a cease-fire. The Israelis were ready, having gained their objectives. The allies, in a panic, got them to evade a quick acceptance, but could not prevent the fall-off of hostilities. By November 5, Israel and Egypt were no longer fighting. Only on that day did the first allied troops appear at the Canal, ostensibly to separate the combatants. By then the only fire to be ceased was theirs against Egyptians.

Hence punishment: our Secretary of the Treasury, George Humphrey, strong in government and close to Eisenhower, gave the British Treasury a virtual ultimatum: as Londoners recall it, he posed the simple choice of an immediate cease-fire or war on the pound, with not a dollar to be had for oil supplies. Unless they heeded the UN, he now would block their path to dollars from the International Monetary Fund, put off their hopes of credit from our Export-Import Bank, and make no effort to align our central bankers behind sterling. If they persisted, they would face a forced devaluation, followed by petrol rationing. His threats were underlined by the week's run on the pound (which he may well have helped along). Humphrey, as they heard him, promised more of the same and worse.

Washington by then was in a hurry. While British forces sailed the ocean, events in Hungary had gone from coup to revolution: the Party's new leadership swung with the wind from the streets, while on the streets good Party members of the old school swung from lampposts. On November 1, Soviet tank columns crossed the border. On November 4, they entered Budapest in force. When British paratroopers first descended on Port Said, Hungarians were fighting block by block. Moscow, meanwhile, hurled threats against Britain and France, rattling rockets at the West's aggression in the Middle East while finishing its restoration in Communist Europe. London and Paris took threats without fuss: deterring the "Bear" was Washington's business. For that very reason, Washington worried. Soviet rocketry was not itself alarming, but a tense, embarrassed Kremlin seemed to pose the risk of war by mutual miscalculation.

This risk, as we have seen in later years, becomes more chilling for the White House (one of the calculators) than for others. To the White House, Suez was a side show, complicating calculations—and a failure to boot.[9]

Besides, the President's accustomed source of counsel also failed just then. The Secretary of State was in the hospital. Dulles had been stricken on November 3 and required a three-hour emergency operation. His available associates seem not to have been viewed with equal confidence. Eisenhower turned to Humphrey.

November 6, our Election Day, was also the first full day of Anglo-French invasion (and a day of mopping up in Budapest). Humphrey's word reached London early in the morning. He set his "ultimatum" to expire that midnight, Greenwich time. Our polls would still be open then, which may have mattered to him.

Reluctantly, the British did as they were told. In a painful morning Cabinet on November 6, they opted for cease-fire. This would leave their forces one-third of the way down the Canal. Two or five or six days more (estimates differed, but their Chiefs of Staff said five or six) would see them in possession of the whole. But for that interval they foresaw many other things; not all are known but some are plain enough: Israeli defection, rage at the UN, preachments from Delhi, Soviet harangues, uproar in Commons, ministerial departures —two already had occurred—and even civil service resignations, each with impact on their own back benches. Capping all, they foresaw ruin for the pound. Looming up behind it were the horrid sights of petrol rationing, devaluation, and repudiated pledges to the sterling bloc. Their cover story, separating the combatants, was moot.

This clinched the argument. Macmillan, with a ministerial case to carry, now became as strong for a cease-fire
as he formerly had been for using force: a dollar-drawing
from the IMF was needed right away; Humphrey would
support it only if his terms were met by midnight.

The Chancellor of the Exchequer rallied a majority.
Eden acquiesced. The time was set for midnight, and
he passed that word to Paris. The French were horrified
but helpless: allied forces had British commanders, and
British troops were in the van on the road south. The
French were too entangled to proceed alone. So they,
too, acquiesced. As others have noted, the Entente-
Cordiale died then and there.

By the time our polls closed the allies had announced
their cease-fire. A few hours later, Eisenhower's re-election was assured. But to his bitter disappointment the
Republicans did not secure majorities in either House of
Congress. His win had been big, but not big enough for
that. Pardonably, if perhaps unreasonably, this added
to his anger at the British, or so it seems.

Momentarily, Eden entertained a gleam of hope. He
and the French still held a "gage," their third of the
Canal, a symbol and a bargaining point. Having done
American bidding and ceased fire, Eisenhower surely
would allow them that and dollars too. Disappointment
followed. Hammarskjold was planning a UN Emergency
Force to post at the Canal, and clear it, and to substitute
for an Israeli occupation of Sinai. Nasser would not let
the UN into Egypt until Britain and France got altogether out. In the circumstances, Washington saw nothing wrong with that: failure should be liquidated fast;
this seemed a kindness. By late November, as the pound

slumped once again and oil supplies grew short, Humphrey resumed arm-twisting. Under pressure, London gave up Eden's "gage." He at least was spared the last surrender. Illness had removed him from the scene, leaving the Leader of the House, R. A. Butler, to preside over the wreckage. Soon Eden resigned in broken health. Acting on advice, the Queen sent not for Butler but for Macmillan.

On November 17, as these last scenes opened, Foreign Secretary Lloyd visited Dulles at his hospital. Their interchange has been reported widely. In one version, Dulles asked him, "Why did you stop?" Lloyd countered, "Why didn't you give us a wink?" Dulles replied "Oh, I couldn't do that." This often has been cited as a nasty sort of joke. Far from it, I take Dulles to have been entirely serious. His words go to the heart of the case. Shortly, I shall try to show you why.

III: The Skybolt Affair

THE SKYBOLT crisis in Anglo-American relations was superficially as sharp as that of Suez, but shorter in duration, smaller in scale, and lesser in consequences. Its public phase erupted only in December 1962 and lasted but three weeks. This episode scarcely is to be compared with Suez as a drama of imperial decline. But it too was an incident in that decline. Indeed, its roots reach to the aftermath of Eden's disappearance from the scene.

I

On taking office at the start of 1957, the new Prime Minister, Macmillan, made it his business to repair relations with Washington. He saw this as a practical imperative for Britain. He evidently also saw it as politically imperative for Tories: within three years their mandate would run out; before the next election Eden's failure had to be erased from their escutcheon. Macmillan needed triumphs in the field where recent failure was most blatant. At the center of that field stood injured pride, and the Americans. Accordingly, he hastened to develop—and to seek symbolic measures of—twin themes. These he was later to articulate as national "independence" and as transatlantic "interdependence." As symbol of the one he chose the British nuclear deterrent, not a bad choice for a man whose government had just displayed its lack of power over real events. As symbol of the other he chose his friendship with Eisenhower.

Macmillan's friend, thoroughly appeased by the withdrawal first of Eden's troops and then of Eden, was responsive on both scores. Eisenhower held the key to both and turned it willingly. In 1957 his Administration sought and shortly gained from Congress an amendment to the Atomic Energy Act, whereby we could share our nuclear technology with Britain. This ended a twelve-year hiatus, deeply resented by successive British Governments, which had begun when Truman severed our initial partnership in ignorance that FDR had pledged continuation. Britain had gone on alone, at great expense, to parallel us first in fission, then in fusion. Now we both were at the very costly stage of marrying atomics to rocketry: the missile age was dawning. Easing Britain's costs by our renewed collaboration eased a lot of consciences in Washington, especially among the men on Roosevelt's wartime team who had so recently administered new punishment to their old friends. Eisenhower seems to have been foremost in that category. Macmillan made the most of it.

But by late 1959, the year Macmillan chose to hold and win a new election, British efforts to take their deterrent into that new age confronted them with shortages alike of funds and space. Surface-to-surface missiles of the sort we were developing—first liquid-fueled, then solid-fueled, eventuating in Minuteman—were an enormous charge upon the British Treasury and also fearful spectres for a crowded island lacking in Great Plains or

Rocky Mountains. Undersea-to-surface missiles of the sort we meant to use with nuclear submarines—Polaris, now Poseidon—were free of land requirements but not of heavy cost, weapons *and* submarines. Besides, the Royal Air Force, quite like our own, despised "sitting in silos." The British aircraft industry, again akin to ours, liked building airplanes. And in the Senior Service, ranking officers were staunch blue-water men, not skulkers undersea, quite like our admirals who so hated Hyman Rickover. Moreover, lacking resources on an American scale, both the RAF and RN could foresee the long-term outcome of homemade equivalents for either Minuteman or Polaris: starvation of all else. (In this events have proved them right; witness their scene today.) Outside these Service ranks were Tory democrats, clamoring for funds with which to play their party's classic trick upon the Opposition: stealing Labour's clothes in education, housing, and the like.

Accordingly, the British Government abandoned plans for surface-to-surface missiles and forebore trying to match us under water. The announcement came soon after the election. This left them short of symbols for Macmillan's themes.

In March 1960, Macmillan met Eisenhower at Camp David, FDR's old "Shangri La" retreat in Maryland. There the PM asked for and received assurance that we would endeavor to develop still another sort of missile, currently in talk-stage: an air-to-surface missile, carried by a bomber for release upon a target 800 miles away. Macmillan also was assured that if we found it technically feasible to make, we would produce it for ourselves and he could then place orders for the RAF. This was the Skybolt missile, so called by our Air Force. The USAF, not to be outdone by the USN, had dreamed it up as a "Polaris of the Sky," and claimed for it a mission of "defense suppression" (clearing paths for SAC), which meant pin-point destruction of ground installations. The British had no interest in this mission but they saw that the same weapon could be used by their own Air Force as a threat to Soviet cities. It might be a decade before the Russians would have means to counter missiles from an aircraft standing off 800 miles, but only some four or five years (it turned out to be even less) before they could strike down high-flying bombers at close range. With Skybolt, the RAF Bomber Command would double its prospective life of proclaimed usefulness as a strategic deterrent. Throughout the 1960s bombers, then, could carry on as symbols of Great Britain's nuclear independence. And London would not have to pay for anything except its missiles as an add-on to our orders, after we brought Skybolt to the production stage.

At the same time that he struck this advantageous bargain, Macmillan pledged to Eisenhower something we were eager to acquire, a European base for nuclear submarines. Macmillan offered, we accepted, Holy Loch in Scotland as our base. Thereby he brought the wrath of many Scots down on his head, along with advocates of unilateral disarmament; nuclear submarines were feared because they might "blow up" and also as a binding tie to us against the Soviets. In offering us Holy Loch Macmillan had to suffer some abuse at home, but he apparently regarded it as cheap at twice the price. For he conceived it as the *quid pro quo* for Skybolt. The two transactions were not linked explicitly. The docu-

ments on each said nothing of the other. But in the
PM's mind the link was real. Eisenhower evidently
thought the same; at least he never publicly disputed
that the two had done a deal.

Thereby Macmillan achieved symbols uniting both
his themes at once, not only Skybolt to suit "independence" but a mutually productive deal to suit "interdependence." The "spirit of Camp David" came to be
his term for both. He frequently invoked it.

But this was 1960. Eisenhower soon would leave the
White House. His replacement might be Kennedy, a
man of different party, temperament, and generation,
Irish to boot. What then of Anglo-American "interdependence"? Moreover, Britain's waning strength
around the world was bound to make her less and less
a partner for Americans in anything but form. This
promised stark dependency a few years hence, or a retreat to puny insularity, should London find no other
source of status. Whence was it to come? Not from
colonies: "winds of change" were blowing. The "Com-
monwealth" still tugged at Tory hearts and minds; its
"multi-racial" version still attracted Labourites; but as
a source of power to fuel status it was unreal.

Sometime in the fall of 1960, Macmillan evidently
made his mind up to reverse a long tradition and take
Britain into "Europe." Whether he decided first and
then persuaded Treasury officials to support him or
vice versa is in question. What is not in question is that
by the spring of 1961 Whitehall was preparing to apply
for Common Market membership; Britain would endeavor to get into the European Economic Community
(and British civil servants, then, should soon manage

to run it). If this ensued, Macmillan would acquire a
third symbol, powerfully reinforcing both the others
or, if need be, as the world changed, ultimately replac-
ing them. Meanwhile, he would try to keep the others
shining bright as interim devices and as reinsurance.
For while he wanted "Europe," he was not disposed to
get it at all costs. Indeed, his subsequent conduct shows
the opposite, that he would risk for Europe neither Tory
unity nor transatlantic ties. He set his mind, apparently,
on sneaking into Europe with all else intact—his primacy
at home and his links with Washington—and acted as a
man who always knew he might not get there. In terms
of British policy the course was revolution, but the
means were Cabinet politics: dilatory, shielded, slow. At
home this proved a brilliant combination: in the space
of only two years, Macmillan's Cabinet colleagues had
choked Europe down. Unfortunately, while they were
about it, de Gaulle across the Channel had averted near
disaster to himself, released France from Algeria, embraced the German Chancellor, and gained sufficient
strength to slam the door of Europe in Macmillan's face.
Macmillan did not get there. But this he would not learn
until December 1962. By then he was embroiled in the
collapse of his Camp David deal.

In 1961, reportedly to his surprise, the PM found
himself quite capable of getting on good terms with our
new President. The generation gap turned out to be no
barrier. Neither did Irish ancestry In temperament, and
taste, and wit, the two were strikingly compatible. So
were their views of the world. Our new Administration
had inherited from Eisenhower's a benign outlook on
Western European unity. This indeed was *de rigeur* in

our post-war bipartisan Establishment. Kennedy would soon proclaim a "grand design" for a transatlantic "partnership" of "equals." He already had the concept well in mind. Its unspoken corollary—so the French suspected —was Britain as our guarantor of a like-minded partner. Macmillan's move toward Europe fitted neatly.

Moreover, Kennedy's new Secretary of Defense—whose intellect, incisiveness, and standing with the President were very visible—seemed less disposed than Eisenhower's to be dubious of Skybolt as a feasible and worthwhile proposition. In the months after Camp David, the outgoing Secretary, Thomas Gates, never an enthusiast, had lost all taste for Skybolt and actually had ordered its development eliminated from the final Eisenhower budget in January 1961.[10] The new Secretary, Robert McNamara, promptly restored it. Macmillan was relieved thereby of having to renegotiate a substitute as his first venture with the new Administration. The narrowness of his escape apparently made him the more hopeful for the future. His new friends now were tied to Skybolt as their own, and more securely, it appeared, than were his old friends. The "spirit of Camp David" had been strengthened, not diminished, by our changeover. He proceeded accordingly, in Parliament and out, to make the most of Skybolt as a symbol. His Secretary of Defence, Harold Watkinson, was wont to brag about it. The PM never stopped him.

II

McNamara had not acted out of special faith or knowledge. Rather it appears that he restored the Skybolt project to the budget partly as a test of technical feasibility and partly because he had need for time to find out whether there impended a real "missile gap" between us and the Soviets (as Democrats had charged in the campaign of 1960). Also, he had thoughts of terminating a more treasured Air Force project, its next-generation strategic bomber, the B-70, a 10 to 15 billion dollar program.

By the time of McNamara's first full budget season, in the fall of 1961, satellite intelligence had stilled talk of a "missile gap." By then also the Budget Bureau, joined by White House scientists, was urging him to pick up Gates's gage and cancel Skybolt. The project had persistently exceeded estimates, stretched out in time, without a better showing than before of its eventual success. But McNamara still was pondering that other cancellation, the B-70, on grounds that new strategic missiles—Minuteman and Polaris—would be fit to do its work before it could be ready. He did not act upon these grounds in budget season, leaving his decision until March (which he was to regret). Possibly in trade, or in the spirit of one-thing-at-a-time, he overrode Executive Office views on Skybolt, and the President consented to keep it underway. Prudently, however, McNamara made a "treaty" with his Air Force Secretary that the cost of its development thereafter would not exceed a fixed dollar amount.

How much of this was understood in London is not clear. Seemingly it all was known but heavily discounted in the light of the budgetary outcome. Besides, a steady stream of reassurances flowed back and forth between the Air Forces. The USAF saw a staunch ally in Her Majesty's Government, and *vice versa*. Also there were the ministrations of our manufacturer, the Douglas Aircraft Corporation, with London representatives in close attendance on the Ministry of Defence. At the start of 1962, Kennedy did throw a frightful scare into Macmillan's son-in-law, then Minister for Air, Julian Amery, by musing at a luncheon about Skybolt's deficiencies. But Amery became so visibly upset that Kennedy, a good host, hastened to reassure him. Since nothing else untoward seemed to happen as the spring advanced, Londoners chose to recall only his reassurance.

In June the British Government was much embarrassed by a commencement speech of McNamara's at Ann Arbor. This was the public version of a private statement he had made to NATO Defense Ministers a month before. Londoners had heard it all before; what was embarrassing was the publicity, not substance. He had aired two of his then most favored concepts: "conventional options" and "controlled response." The first called for more men-at-arms in Europe. London acquiesced, provided none of them were British; no embarrassment in that. The second concept called for "integration," centralized direction, of nuclear deterrents in NATO as a whole. London's own deterrent, although "independent," was within this rubric: under longstanding arrangements Bomber Command's targeting conformed to plans of our Strategic Air Command. This second concept was what made for trouble. British Ministers did not think McNamara aimed at them. Indeed he did not (or not directly): mainly he had Paris in his mind; from where he stood the British nuclear deterrent, although wasteful of resources and symbolically a nuisance, was not independent in its use, hence operationally no problem. But McNamara's strictures on the foolishness of separate nuclear forces were grabbed up by Labourites and thrown in Tory faces. Watkinson had hard times in the House. To appease him, McNamara publicly avowed that he had not meant Britain. Tory Ministers went back to sleep, although perhaps less comfortably than heretofore.

Still, as they discovered later, the spring of 1962 proved fatal for the Skybolt project. By July, McNamara had concluded his first, hard congressional fight, had faced down Air Force friends there, and had terminated the B-70. Despite his urging, Congress actually appropriated new funds for that aircraft, never mind that he had chosen to withdraw them from the budget after its initial presentation. McNamara then had said he would not spend the funds and Kennedy had formally impounded them, taking on themselves the onus of eventual demise for the manned bomber. McNamara and his Controller, Charles Hitch, evidently learned from this how hard it was to stop an Air Force project in which Congress had sunk funds for many years. They also learned, it seems, how relatively advantageous it would be to have such projects cancelled and the budget-line removed before Congress could debate future financing.

Also by July, continued funding for that other project, Skybolt, had made plain beyond a doubt that its development would far exceed the ceiling set in McNamara's "treaty." The cost curve, month-by-month, appeared conclusive on this score. At the same time, there was good news from a different Air Force front: Minuteman's development was now ahead of schedule; the weapon soon would go into production.

Before the end of August 1962, McNamara's technical
and budgetary aides were urging him to do what Budget
Bureau sources had proposed a year before, namely to
cancel Skybolt. By now they could present him a full
argument on grounds of cost-effectiveness: development
was slow, expensive, and unpromising. By all accounts
the trouble centered on a guidance system accurate
enough to meet the mission of defense-suppression. Some
advisers evidently thought this unachievable. At any
rate, it would cost more than it was worth. For finishing
the job through full production, the estimate was now
$2.5 billion over three successive fiscal years. We had
alternatives: for the short term we could use another air-
to-surface missile with a simpler guidance system and a
shorter range, the Hound Dog; in the longer term, the
mission of defense-suppression would be moot, as Minuteman took over from manned bombers. Money spent
on Skybolt could be better spent on speeding up the
takeover, or saved. As for deterrence (Britain's use of
Skybolt) Minuteman could meet our needs in combination with Polaris.

This is the logic McNamara made his own some two
months later during the next budget season. Before then
he did not decide: no need. Instead he waited on events
or arguments that might persuade him otherwise. Apparently, none came his way.

III

In September 1962, a new British Secretary of Defence
made his first trip in that capacity to Washington. This
was Peter Thorneycroft, previously Minister of Aviation.

His promotion followed from "Macmillan's Purge" during July when seven senior Ministers—Watkinson among them—were shoved off the front bench to put a "new face" on the Government, now entering a mid-term time of troubles with constituents. Thorneycroft was not a stranger to the front bench. He had sat there before with a still loftier portfolio as Chancellor of the Exchequer. But in 1959 he had resigned on a "matter of principle" (money), which won him some respect but not a following from Tories. After that year's election, Macmillan had let him back into office, but not Cabinet. Now, by all accounts, he was delighted to return there. He had force, drive, and ambition to employ there. He also had ideas. More than most of his colleagues he was oriented toward Europe. Indeed he was a Europe-firster. The American connection was for him a thing of reason, not of wartime memories or emotion.

Thorneycroft was well received in Washington. He made a good impression. He in turn was well impressed by McNamara and by McNamara's standing with the President. He saw them both at length. Thorneycroft had Skybolt on his mind, of course—also perhaps Ann Arbor—but heard nothing to alarm him on that score. McNamara did allude with feeling to uncertainties and cost in its development. But this was an old story for the former Minister of Aviation; such things always seemed to take longer and cost more than expected. Besides, in English ears, a guidance system did not sound like a great trouble; British purposes required only that the Russians think the weapon could be guided to a city. Thorneycroft took care to stress that British defense posture was dependent on the weapon, and let it go at that. By all accounts, he went home stimulated by his contacts and unruffled on the score of Skybolt.

But by mid-October McNamara seems to have made up his mind that Skybolt ought to go. This was not altogether lost on London. Unofficial sources brought disturbing hints both to the British Embassy and to the Defence Ministry. Thereupon the Cuban missile crisis intervened and pushed all else aside for two climatic weeks. "Budget season" virtually stopped still.

In the first week of November, McNamara found time to pick up the threads on Skybolt. He had an oblique inquiry from Thorneycroft which should not be left dangling. If the weapon were to go the British would have trouble—that was plain enough—and might want us to help resolve it. The sooner they found out, the longer they would have to think about their problem, and its terms of resolution, and the help they sought from us. The sooner they took thought, the sooner we would find out what they wanted.

But at the outset of November McNamara could not tell them Skybolt was to die, no matter that he had decided so, for this was not yet an Administration decision. He was just then sending to our Joint Chiefs of Staff, for comment, the conclusions of his own civilian staff in which he shared. The JCS response would be forthcoming in two weeks. No doubt it would be favorable to Skybolt: the Air Force could rely on interservice comity (you support my system, I support yours).[11] Then JCS opinions and his own, on the whole defense budget, were to be submitted for decision by the President in conference with his chief White House and Budget Bureau aides. The conference date was tentatively set for Thanksgiving, three weeks hence. The President might opt for McNamara's view but he could not do so in form until Thanksgiving, lest referral to the Chiefs appear a mockery. How then were the British to have time for thought? The President's decisions would be sent down to the Services with strict injunctions against publication before January's Budget Message. But controversial ones were almost sure to leak within a week or so of their receipt. London scarcely could collect its thoughts amidst publicity. The British would have to be warned.

McNamara took that teaser to the White House. On November 7 he saw the President, together with the Secretary of State, Dean Rusk, and Kennedy's Assistant, McGeorge Bundy. Meeting in the aftermath of Cuba, they were happy with each other and receptive to him. On his showing they agreed that Skybolt ought to go, and also that the British must be warned without delay. Being "clever chaps," as someone said, they no doubt would find ways around their problem, once alerted, and would tell us what, if anything, they wanted us to do. As for the mechanics of a warning, McNamara volunteered to handle it. The others were content. These four had more pressing matters on their minds. For one, the Chinese were marching against India. For another, Khrushchev's missiles might be gone from Cuba, but his bombers still had to be taken out of there. Those issues occupied more time and thought than Skybolt. That, after all, was no longer their problem: what remained was rather for those clever chaps to ponder. They would now be warned.

McNamara lost no time in summoning the British

Ambassador, Sir David Ormsby Gore. Then, by pre-arrangement, after Embassy dispatches had reached London, McNamara telephoned to Thorneycroft. In neither case could our man say to them definitively that Skybolt would be stopped. But what he could do was make plain to them his own strong disposition. He also could assure them, and he did, that when the time came to decide, we would consult with them, and on next steps, before announcing anything. He undertook to do this personally within a month. He would come to London to see Thorneycroft.

McNamara's auditors both knew their man. They evidently took it that he meant to kill the project even if he were unable yet to say so. Both in response and in his cables home, Gore apparently expressed himself appalled. Thorneycroft's response was relatively calm: if Skybolt's cancellation were to follow then the British must go on to something else. He is said to have dropped the word "Polaris," among others, and hung up the telephone. Thorneycroft's calm soothed McNamara, who assumed thereafter that the British chaps were working on their problem.

Gore's dispatches were read in the Foreign Office, naturally, and at Admiralty House, Macmillan's temporary residence (10 Downing Street was then under repair), and by Thorneycroft. Despite the latter's calm, their news was hardly welcome in those quarters, least of all to the PM, and it went nowhere else. Macmillan soon would swallow down still more disturbing news of Tory disappointment in six by-elections. July's "new look" scarcely had been enough. He also was enduring, week-by-week, a dreary round of argument in Cabinet on agricultural concessions to the Common Market. Britain-into-Europe offered him a new face capable of covering all else. He once had hoped to have it the preceding August. Cabinet foot-dragging on agriculture had precluded that, and was not yet quite overcome. Meanwhile, the noises out of a resurgent Paris were discouraging. Macmillan did not hanker after trouble now with Washington. Skybolt had survived before, why not again? Promised consultation was to be at second-level. There remained a higher level; Kennedy had not invoked it. If this were the end for Skybolt surely Kennedy would call him; in the absence of a call perhaps the end was not assured; McNamara was not the sole power in the Pentagon.

Reasoning on some such grounds, Macmillan asked that Gore seek from the White House some procedural assurances: no interim publicity ahead of consultation and no final action until after. A week before Thanksgiving Kennedy acceded cheerfully. As I understand it, Macmillan also queried whether his Ambassador thought he need call the President. In advance of that holiday Gore is said to have thought not; thereafter McNamara would come over to consult. The PM evidently saw no point in telephoning prematurely. Meanwhile, Thorneycroft, for his part, waited on events. He evidently took it that a man as smart as McNamara would not trouble to consult if he intended but to snatch away one missile without offering another. Thorneycroft seems also to have thought that on the telephone he had conveyed to McNamara a sufficient clue. No wonder Thorneycroft was calm; on those presumptions he could well afford to be. Also he had no need to take thought.

What was there to think about? He simply had to wait for our man's offer.

McNamara evidently had conceived that were he in the other's shoes he probably would opt for Polaris. And although he was counting on the British to take thought, he could not resist doing some of their work for them. He set certain of his staffers to consider how we might help Thorneycroft. His staffers then consulted colleagues in our State Department. There they found an almost frantic opposition to Polaris for the British. Whereas Skybolt could not have prolonged the life of Britain's airborne nuclear deterrent much past 1969, Polaris might suffice a submarine force through the 1970s. What sort of an example would this convey to those other seekers after nuclear forces, so scorned at Ann Arbor? What would such evidence of our "special relationship" convey about the British as potential Europeans? What mischief might this do the cause of Common Market membership for Britain? Behind such questions loomed the spectre of de Gaulle.

State Department staffers pressed these questions on their counterparts across the river. They pressed them, too, on Rusk, and drafted for his signature instructions limiting what McNamara might convey in consultation. He could give the British Skybolt as it then was, for completion at their risk and their expense, or let them hang Hound Dog under their bombers. Polaris and its submarines were out of bounds. Rusk and McNamara had dealt seriously face to face in different terms, and would again. But Rusk did not choose to deny his staff their Secretary's signature. And McNamara did not choose to fuss. There would be time enough for that once Thorneycroft had asked—as logically he would do —for Polaris. And if by chance he should not ask, so much the better. The State Department's alternatives would then suffice.

Early in November, McNamara had intended a quick trip to London soon after Thanksgiving. At that holiday budget conference everything went true to form, and Skybolt cancellation was decided, subject to consultation with the British. Everybody present, McNamara included, seems to have assumed that he would fly to London very shortly. But other issues intervened, and he put off the trip from day to day. The likelihood of leaks seems to have faded from his mind. He was pledged to be in Paris on December 12 for a long-scheduled NATO ministerial meeting. For convenience he eventually decided to roll two trips into one and stop at London the preceding day. By then the budgetary wheels had turned, procedures had been followed, and the usual had happened: Skybolt cancellation leaked into the press December 7.

By December 11, when McNamara reached London, the place was in an uproar.[12] He did not improve the public look of things by criticizing Skybolt to the press as he deplaned. Soon after, he and Thorneycroft began their consultation.

What ensued was "a Pinero drama of misunderstanding," as Arthur Schlesinger described it in *A Thousand Days*.[13] The reasons are not far to seek: Thorneycroft was waiting for an offer of Polaris; McNamara was expecting him to ask for it. What McNamara offered was a crushing disappointment, and offensive to boot. How, as Henry Brandon notes, could Englishmen base "independence" upon something labeled Hound Dog? What Thorneycroft eventually was induced to ask he couched exclusively in terms of principles, no homework behind them, not a trace of cost-effectiveness analysis: would we publicly back Britain's nuclear independence, never mind the ways and means? McNamara's instructions barred an affirmative answer. He exceeded his instructions by implying that Polaris pledged to NATO might be feasible. Thorneycroft was having none of that. Polaris once in Britain's hands could be pledged if she liked; this was independence. But the pledge could not be a condition-precedent. There were no such on Skybolt. Symbolically these had to be equivalent, or else we were betraying the Alliance, breaching the spirit of Camp David, ratting on our deal. What then of Holy Loch? What then, indeed, of our entire relationship?

Understandably, suspicion mounted on both sides. Thorneycroft was playing to a gallery, as McNamara found out when he read the evening papers. But Thorneycroft was also in dead earnest. He felt betrayed. His expectations had been overthrown. What reason could there be for this save enmity, shades of Ann Arbor? McNamara's feelings were not altogether different. He too had been surprised, and then lambasted. Was this the prelude to Tory Gaullism? Did it presage an Anglo-French adventure despite us? How could Thorneycroft have done so little homework? And why? Was he trying to disrupt our whole relationship?

The next week was a crowded time for both these men, and also for their chiefs. The NATO ministerial meeting, a three-day affair, opened in Paris on December 12, Defense and Foreign Ministers attending. Mac-

millan had two scheduled conferences that week, first
with de Gaulle at Rambouillet, December 15, then with
Kennedy at Nassau, starting the 18th. None of these
sessions had been set with Skybolt in mind. The timing
was coincidental. Rambouillet had been planned as an
exercise in Anglo-French relations on the eve of British
agricultural concessions to the Common Market. Nassau
had been planned as a relaxing session of good friends,
prelude to Christmas, one among the semiannual meetings which Macmillan had begun with Ike and carried
on with JFK: symbols of interdependence. Now Nassau
had to be, as Rambouillet was sure to be, an altogether
serious affair. Macmillan and Kennedy would take up
where Thorneycroft and McNamara left off.

Meanwhile, they were assured a crisis atmosphere. The
British press grew more indignant day by day, fueled
by Defence and aviation sources, dramatizing Thorneycroft as David against Goliath. In Commons the suspi-
cions sown by Suez—and Ann Arbor—shot above the
surface: Tory rightists fulminated; Labourites jeered.
On our side Congress had adjourned; the press had not
(nor had our Air Force, to say nothing of the Douglas
Corporation). London's indignation was a major story.[14]
The *Washington Post* attacked the Kennedy Administration editorially for letting London down; in words
and tone that editorial invoked the whole weight of
bipartisan-establishment opinion. For emphasis the paper's publisher called privately on Kennedy: did he, the
narrowly elected Democrat, intend to break an Eisenhower bargain with our staunchest friends?

The President was puzzled by the crisis. If London's
situation was so serious why had there been no phone

call from Macmillan? Kennedy knew very well that he
had meant no harm to Britain; he also had no taste for
seeming to have done so in the eyes of well-connected
publishers. But neither did he want to risk a saving of
$2.5 billion; and by now he had no taste for Skybolt on
its merits. Yet he was sensitive to State Department
arguments against a substitution of Polaris: Britain-
into-Europe had the first priority, not only for his "grand
design" but for Macmillan too. Why risk appearances
that cut against this grain? The President thus had to
square a circle. And he had to do it by December 18.

Before emplaning for the Nassau Conference Kennedy
consulted McNamara and Rusk as each returned from
Paris. The three had reached the same conclusion: there
was nothing for it but an offer of Polaris made condi-
tional upon commitment by the British that their new
deterrent force would be at NATO's beck and call, not
used alone, thus easing charges that we favored Britain
above France or Germany. Thorneycroft already had
rejected such a concept out of hand, but Kennedy and
Rusk had not been there to hear him, while his auditor
may not have felt the weight of politics behind his words.
McNamara, indeed, seems previously to have thought
Polaris-with-a-NATO-tie equivalent to Skybolt. Only
now did he review the fine print from Camp David.

Kennedy had offered space in his own plane to Gore,
the British Ambassador, who not so incidentally was a
friend. Once they were in the air the two began a tête-à-
tête, examining the circle Kennedy must square by the
light of Macmillan's problem. At the heart of that problem was politics, the symbol of "independence." Kennedy
the politician saw it plainly when his friend, also a man

of politics, explained it. Polaris tied to NATO could not meet the case. But a straight substitution of Polaris for Skybolt raised the risks of which State staffers warned. Thereupon these two men improvised a new scheme: Kennedy would offer to continue Skybolt in development, not for ourselves but for the British, with a fifty-fifty split of costs. Thereby we would lose part of our prospective saving, but we would have shown support for British independence without any of the risks attendant on Polaris. With Macmillan very shortly to be faced, the money mattered rather less to Kennedy than it had done before. Besides, he still would save more than a billion dollars in production funds. Immediately on deplaning, Gore is said to have gone off with the Prime Minister and tried this out on him. Macmillan evidently would have none of it. It came at least one day too late.

The night before, December 17, Americans had watched their President on television in a year-end interview with correspondents, taped the preceding day. Kennedy's performance ranks among his best; his answers to all questions had been thoughtful and adroit. One set of questions concerned Skybolt. The President's response was definitive. A month before his budget presentation he provided in short compass a well-argued brief against continuing the weapon for our purposes, including its deficiencies and our alternatives. Thus, deliberately it seems, he locked the door on Skybolt cancellation. Macmillan learned of this only as he reached Nassau, hours before Kennedy, and on deplaning had a text of that response thrust at him by a member of the press. Thereafter the Prime Minister apparently

struck his once-treasured weapon from his mind. As he
is said to have remarked on the next day, Skybolt was
no longer the least use to him: the lady had been violated in public.

Londoners at Nassau were a tense and angry lot. Macmillan had brought with him a strong Cabinet delegation. Thorneycroft was there along with the then Earl
of Home and Duncan Sandys, the Foreign and Colonial
Secretaries. A large press delegation swarmed around
them. The mood, in Henry Brandon's words, was one
of "nagging exasperation and bitter indignation . . . such
as I have never experienced in all the Anglo-American
conferences I have covered over the past twenty years."[15]

Macmillan may well have been less indignant than
the rest, but he had every reason for exasperation. Three
days earlier, at Rambouillet, he had been all but told
that France would bar his way to Europe. De Gaulle,
aloof and cold, reportedly had lectured him at length on
reasons why the British were unready to be Europeans.
In London this was seen as a French declaration of intent
to work against their membership in the EEC. De Gaulle,
indeed, had ostentatiously invited them to drop their
bid for membership and seek a lesser form of association.
Macmillan had demurred, had pressed his case, and possibly to signify his Europeanness had told of his intention
to maintain an independent nuclear deterrent. Reportedly he had said he would seek to retain Skybolt, or to
substitute Polaris, or at worst would build his own just
as de Gaulle was doing. Macmillan may have meant,
thereby, to open prospects of collaboration in the nuclear
sphere, once he too was inside the Common Market.
De Gaulle, however, had made no response.

Against this backdrop, the Prime Minister now faced
the President. When their conference opened formally
on the 19th, Kennedy first advanced his "fifty-fifty"
scheme. Macmillan was unmoved. Kennedy then tried
another late improvisation, this one from a State Department source, urging a joint study on next steps in British
weaponry to be concluded before Parliament returned
from Christmas Recess. By then the shape of EEC negotiations might be plain, which would remove a lot of
present risks. Macmillan brushed aside delay and pressed
for an immediate solution. Thereupon the President
was forced back on an earlier idea: Polaris tied to
NATO. Macmillan responded with an eloquent solil-
oquy. Its flavor can be gleaned from a close reading of
accounts by Brandon and Schlesinger. Its point was
buried in a reference to the Queen's prerogative of using
British weapons independently at moments of supreme
emergency. On this the two sides built a compromise,
the so-called Nassau Agreement.

By that Agreement, reached after two days of bargaining, the British were to get from us Polaris missiles;
they would build the needed submarines, also the
nuclear warheads, with our technical assistance under
previous agreements. They pledged this weaponry to
NATO from the outset, in a multinational force—to
which we also would contribute—under integrated command. The pledge was permanent, an irreversible commitment. But it contained an emergency escape clause.
In a time of supreme peril to Great Britain, these submarines could be withdrawn, temporarily of course, for
independent use by HMG. Integration thus was mar-
ried to a form of independence.

Macmillan was enormously relieved by this result and went home in a mood of triumph. Britain still would have a nuclear deterrent and he still could claim that it was independent. The British press, however, was inclined to jeer: he came home shorn of Skybolt with a new, expensive weapon tied to NATO. What had happened to the fighting-spirit of a week before? Broken by the Americans? Kennedy did not share this reaction. He knew the British had got more from him than he had wished to give. But he and his immediate associates were heartened by the thought that Nassau's formula might be extended to the French.

De Gaulle had long sought nuclear assistance from us, but had held out against any form of integration. Might he not accept this form: NATO *cum* escape-clause? He did not yet have the wherewithal to build his own warheads and submarines. But we could give him that, and spare France the endeavor on her own, if he too would commit his weaponry to NATO in this fashion. On American insistence, the Nassau conferees had cabled him an invitation into the new NATO force; this held the prospect of assistance equalizing French with British nuclear technology. The British conferees had not been much enthused in the cold aftermath of Rambouillet. But our men, knowing nothing about that, were hopeful of De Gaulle's response.[16] Kennedy apparently was ready for a long negotiation with the French which might result, over much Senate opposition, in London's sharing of our nuclear technology with Paris, thus rendering Polaris useable for France.

De Gaulle appears, however, to have read the British press. Moreover, through a comedy of diplomatic errors he got contradictory signals about Kennedy's intentions. Besides, he had no use for NATO; its symbols warred with those he held most dear in his own politics. And as a dramatist he evidently knew a good stage when he saw one: the Nassau Agreement, cozily arranged by "Anglo-Saxons," offered opportunity for frontally assaulting Britain's aims in Europe. On January 14, 1963, he held a press conference. In well-rehearsed responses to set questions he announced that France would veto British membership in the EEC, restating his remarks at Rambouillet, and also that he had no interest in our Nassau offer. France would build her own deterrent for herself: true independence.

Thereby Kennedy received a crucial setback to his "grand design," while McNamara lost some crucial ground in arguing "controlled response," to say nothing of nonproliferation. Macmillan, at the same time, was deprived of "Europe." For him this was a great strategic loss, but not without some tactical compensation. When Parliament resumed late in January, anger at de Gaulle displaced suspiciousness of a "sell-out" over Skybolt. Kennedy's indictment of the weapon, now much quoted, helped as well. Kennedy, for his part, also had some compensation: Congress made no move to counter Skybolt's cancellation.

IV: Crisis Behavior

AS HISTORY may read them, Suez and Skybolt are unlike. Especially is this the case in British terms, where one was an event of enduring significance, the other a mere episode.[17] Yet despite all differences of symbolism, timing, issues, outcomes, the same pattern of behavior runs through both. Let us pause over this pattern. It has much to tell about the task of maintaining friendly relations—at least between such friends as Washington and London.

My previous chapters make the pattern plain. It is woven from four strands: muddled perceptions, stifled communications, disappointed expectations, paranoid reactions. In turn, each "friend" misreads the other, each is reticent with the other, each is surprised by the other, each replies in kind. A spiral starts, and only when the one bows low before the other's *latest* grievance does the spiral stop. That spiral rose much higher over Suez than over Skybolt, which testifies mainly to Kennedy's detachment. Had his ego been as much engaged as Eisenhower's or his stakes as high, or had he felt committed to his Europeanists, Nassau would have set off a new turn.

I

What explains the crisis pattern? Why do governments so closely linked engage in such behavior? These are my questions for this chapter. Answers bring us a long way toward understanding what may be the hazards for our government when it endeavors to pursue its aims by means of a peacetime alliance.

Personalities afford a partial answer, often taken for the whole. As such it warms the hearts of journalists and diarists, and devil-theorists everywhere. In many English memories and memoirs, "Suez" is spelled "Dulles," the self-righteous-devious-schemer. Americans quite often spell it "Eden," the illusioned-nervous-fumbler. Far be it from me to downgrade the impact of human personality on governmental conduct. But obviously this is insufficient to explain repetitive behavior of successive human beings. Indeed it does not suffice even for the same men in successive contexts. No doubt the personalities of Dulles and Eden—in reality, not caricature—contributed to the severity of Suez. So did their lack of empathy for one another. But Macmillan and Kennedy are quite another matter, while Thorneycroft and McNamara started on the best of terms. Yet the Suez pattern is discernible in Skybolt. By contrast, before 1956 Eden had made do with Dulles (and *vice-versa*) on numerous occasions where that pattern does not show.

Divergences of policy afford another explanation, comforting for those diplomatists and theorists who reify the State into a single calculator, rationally pursuing its determinate self-interest. But this is no more a sufficient

answer than the last. Policies there no doubt were in
London and in Washington. One can, at least, find trend
lines in their actions over time and label each a policy
by hindsight. But trends of action emanating from these
capitals run parallel, in most respects, both before 1956
and before 1962. Differences in emphasis exist, of course,
also in effort applied. There are, however, no discern-
able divergences of trends so wide as to account for the
collision we experienced in each of those two years. Nor
are there signs that either side deliberately intended
quarrelling with the other. Quite the contrary, they both
espoused and actually pursued the policy of keeping company with one another. Their actions toward each other
ran on trend lines of successive compromises and accom-
modations, not least regarding Egypt during 1954 and
nuclear weaponry in 1960. The crises in these spheres
thus broke the trend in their relations, belying this aspect of policy, not reinforcing it. And outcomes in both
cases show how unprepared they were for that. These
crises came upon them as bolts from the blue. Deliberate
intention? Far from it.

Another partial explanation lies in orders of priority.
Both governments took actions of all sorts in many
spheres at once, pursuing many things besides accommodation with each other. Each crisis shows divergence of
priorities. Nasser and his Canal, Moscow and its threats,
Bomber Command and its deterrent, Paris and the EEC,
even the "special relationship" itself were not viewed
quite alike by Washington and London. Out of these
shades of difference they derived a different weighting
for one sphere as against others. But differences of these
sorts occur all the time. A government's priorities derive

from resources, geography, and public moods, and from the life experience of those who rule, together with the history they learned at school. From Washington to London different orders of priority are commonplace. Yet we do not have a crisis every day. The question remains, why the behavior in these crises? If personalities and policy are not sufficient answers, neither are established orders of priority.

This brings us to the rationality of individual decisions, to the good sense, or its absence, in a given act of choice. Had Dulles but backed SCUA with the wherewithal for boycott, or had Eden but insisted on a better war plan, or Macmillan on a simpler weapon, or had McNamara but deferred his cancellation, it is likely that these crises would have blown away or never come at all. Yet the reasonableness of each such choice is readily defended. Considering American conditions, the Secretary of the Treasury could not pledge dollars for a boycott while Egyptians safely piloted our ships through the Canal, whence shippers much preferred to go. Considering British unprepardeness, Musketeer was a triumph of improvisation—also of coordination—executed well and failing technically in only one respect: blockage of the Canal. Considering intended British uses, Skybolt appeared to have no major flaw except the need for guidance to city-sized targets, a relatively modest technical requirement; besides, it was the cheapest thing in sight and kept the Navy quite as happy as the Air Force. Considering the American budgetary process, Skybolt's cancellation in December was a coup: exclusion from the January budget left its friends on stony ground where they must lobby for an increase, rather than against a cut, should they appeal from President to Congress.

The case for the defense goes deeper still. Beneath these reasonable surfaces lie virtual necessities: imperatives of bureaucratic politics. On each occasion—and not these alone—no better way was open to the man who made the choice, in light of his relations with his governmental colleagues. Dulles had to do his best for Eisenhower's peace, and also for the Eisenhower budget of which Humphrey was a guardian. Especially was Humphrey guardian of credits under Treasury control. Eden had to satisfy his activists within the terms set by his generals. These emphatically included sea-borne landings. Macmillan had to base his nuclear symbol on a durable consensus both in Cabinet and among his Services. What better than a weapon which caused no one harm? McNamara had to cancel Skybolt or risk cumulative loss of $2.5 billion in successive fiscal years. Immediate action held the key to Air Force and congressional acquiescence.

For these men, I have said, no better way was open. Theoretically, each had the option to give up. But this they were determined not to do. Dulles was determined to hang on to Eden's coattails. Eden was determined to have Nasser's head, or at least save his own. Macmillan was determined to remain a member of the Nuclear Club. Kennedy, with McNamara, wanted all that money. Eden and Macmillan had their lives at stake, politically, at least in their own estimations. Dulles had at stake his credit with his President. Kennedy was only after money, which goes far to show why Skybolt is the lesser of these crises. But the money mattered to him; otherwise there would have been no crisis.

Americans may boggle at my claims for Musketeer. Englishmen may find our budgeting incomprehensible. Never mind for now; I soon shall have occasion to elaborate.

Meanwhile, where does this leave us? It leaves us with a clue: what seemed "cockeyed" from abroad was rational when viewed in terms of home.

II

Foreign relations begin at home. What went wrong in those instances—and others of the sort—was their external impact, *not* their inner logic. The makers of these choices did not err in their own terms. Rather, their choices ran afoul of someone else's terms. The fatal flaw in SCUA was not lack of teeth to monitor Egyptian management, but rather London's passion to unseat that management (and Nasser too). The fatal flaw in Musketeer was not its time schedule as such, but rather the effect of a delay in Washington. The fatal flaw in Skybolt was not British uses but American requirements. The one thing wrong with McNamara's budgeting was Thorneycroft's desire—and Macmillan's—for a quiet life.

Did not the makers of those choices see what they were courting overseas? They saw the "big picture" but blurred fine details. Dulles saw that Eden wanted war, he spent months trying to stop him. Having got him well entangled in UN negotiations Dulles evidently thought he had him stopped. Eden saw of course—how could he help it—that Washington was eager for a peaceful outcome. But "Ike" would "lie doggo" until election; besides, he would be conscious of analogies to Panama.

Macmillan knew, even in 1960, that topside at the Pentagon there was no little skepticism about Skybolt. But he had done his "deal," implicit though it was; the tactics that achieved it should suffice to keep it. McNamara knew very well that cancellation could make trouble for the British. But they were "clever chaps." When they had worked it out he would be helpful.

Not only did these men have blurry vision when they looked abroad, but also they took sightings by the kindly light of hope. Dulles evidently thought "public opinion" spurred by Labour opposition weakened Eden's hand. Eden evidently thought that lying doggo meant a passivity extending even to Ike's jaws. Macmillan evidently thought our Chiefs of Staff might be a match for McNamara, even as they had been for his predecessors. McNamara, in turn, apparently supposed that Thorneycroft's reaction would be like his own had trouble been reversed. Hopes like these abounded in both crises. By no means were they confined to these instances alone.

In this there are two ironies. For one, each hopeful estimate of friends abroad was grown at home, rooted in the inner politics of home; indeed it was the only estimate consistent with the chosen course of action. In effect, these men saw what they had to see if what they felt they had to do stood any chance to work. And second, what they chose to do turned out to be in fact the one thing that their friends found hardest to endure in their terms, their own politics, not as perceived across the water but as actually pursued by them.

I offer you these ironies as further clues. Again they point us toward concerns at home. In terms of home, what suited "A" the best hurt "B" the worst. So Eden,

by October 1956, saw no way to his war save Musketeer
under Israeli cover, which precluded sailings while the
lid went on. He estimated—probably correctly—that his
transatlantic friends would acquiesce in a *fait accompli*.
But the one thing Eisenhower saw no way to do was acquiesce in something that remained undone. So Dulles
earlier scaled SCUA's teeth to Humphrey's size, while
Eden, who had bought it, then confronted colleagues
all of whom felt "sold." So with McNamara and Thorneycroft in Schlesinger's "Pinero drama of misunderstanding." So later with Macmillan reading Kennedy's
TV remarks on Skybolt: "The lady had been violated
in public."

No wonder the behavior patterns we are probing show
successive expectations crowned by disappointment, with
surprise inducing paranoid reactions. The expectations
suited felt necessities. The disappointment ran to treasured projects. The surprise was genuine. The pain was
real. And the suspicion was commensurate. How could
such harm be caused by inadvertence? Above all from a
friend: "How could he do that to me?" This was the
plaint, in turn, of Eden, Dulles, Eisenhower, Thorneycroft, McNamara, Macmillan, and even Kennedy. It is
easy to see why.

What then of reticence, another thread through both
our crises? What accounts for the successive spells of
stifled communication? Clearly these contributed to
faulty expectations, hence to unintended pain. Why
should communications fail between allies so sorely
needing to guess right about each other? To answer is
to offer one more clue.

The summaries before you show an evident evasive-

ness on our side in the first two months of Suez: Dulles
weaves and bobs. Then there is Eden's turn to the UN
without informing Dulles, followed by the blackout in
October 1956 on word of what the British meant to do
with France and Israel. And in the Skybolt case there is
the silence between Thorneycroft and McNamara—to
say nothing of others—which lasted for five weeks.

Superficially, these instances are of two sorts, one
turning on embarrassment, the other on retaliation. But
beneath these motives we find others, less obvious. Those
others seem to have a common source: between London
and Washington the wall of sovereignty was full of holes.

How could McNamara unveil his plans to Thorneycroft with assurance that the RAF would not learn and
so inform the USAF before he wanted his subordinates
to know of his decision? Or *vice versa*? How could Eden
whisper into Eisenhower's ear plans he was keeping
secret from his permanent officials, to say nothing of
his Parliament and press? Eden feared, reportedly, that
Eisenhower surely would turn Dulles loose to badger
him again. Behind that fear presumably lay an awareness that our State Department would arouse his Foreign
Office regulars; these at the very least. Badgering from
Dulles would be seconded at home, and thereby mag-
nified.

If Dulles, for his part, was less than candid at an
earlier stage, consider the embarrassments of candor.
He walked a tightrope in London. Presumably he did
so because he was walking a tightrope at home. For him
to bare his breast in Eden's company might have been
most imprudent, and not only for the reason that they
did not like each other. Dulles worked for Eisenhower

and was dependent on him. Eden had been Eisenhower's friend for many years. Besides, there was a telephone from Downing Street to 1600 Pennsylvania Avenue. Should Dulles have counseled in August that the President never would countenance force? But Nasser might yet run amok. Or should Dulles have "winked" in October, as Lloyd later asked? But "peace" was the word at the White House. On the merits it is hard to see what candor could have offered; certainly not signals of this sort. And signals of whatever sort could get back to the White House not as Dulles phrased them but as Eden recalled them; whether in complaint or thanks he might pick up that telephone.

In an alliance such as this the membrane between sovereign states is paper-thin and porous. Transatlantic reticence is of a piece with reticence at home. For any word to friends across the ocean may come back to other ears at home. As well, a word to friends at home may skip across the water. The relationship is reciprocal. Either way the motive is the same; prudence counsels reticence.

The stifling of communication in these instances afforded self-protection to the men who did it, protection for their causes and accordingly for them. They were guarding exposed flanks—their own. And what they had to guard against was not only 3,000 miles away, far from it: their exposed positions offered targets to associates, the threat was at close quarters. These men of reticence were vulnerable at home. Their vulnerability becomes a final clue. It points us in the same direction as the other clues: toward the bureaucratic politics of home.

III

How then are we to characterize the hazards in relations between governments like Washington and London? Plainly we begin with an acknowledgment that these hazards arise out of necessitous relations *inside* governments.

What do our clues show? They show each side comprised of men intent upon their own concerns, and upon negotiation to advance them—Londoners with Londoners, Washingtonians with Washingtonians. Their self-absorption is a day-and-night affair; it never flags. They calculate accordingly and act to suit. So do their counterparts inside the other government. From one side to the other, awareness filters through their self-absorption. Comprehension of the other's actual behavior is a function of their own concerns. What occurs across the water tends to register in terms of its effects upon their calculations. So with perception of the other side's concerns. What they see across the water tends to be a virtual projection of those calculations. Habituated to regard the other side as friendly, they habitually expect accommodation for themselves. When both sides happen to produce compatible outcomes, or when one sees reason to adjust in its own terms, the alliance "works." When mutual expectations turn out to be mutually exclusive, crisis follows: thus it was in 1956 and 1962.

What made these allies crisis-prone was not the high priority they gave their own concerns. All governments do that at every time. The men inside each government have grown up there, gained power there, and exercise it there. They will retain or lose it there. Moreover, they are governing a nation, and their sense of obligation turns upon the task as so defined. These men did not propel themselves toward crisis when they registered the other side's behavior only as it bore on their concerns. In Washington and London men who govern draw their pay for this. At any given time these men deal first with what they must deal next. Priorities are set by their own business. What happens on the other side deserves attention when and as it bears upon their business. All else is tourism. No one is paid for that except researchists and diplomatists, who do not govern. So it always is, yet there is not always a crisis.

Crises were brought on by the next step in their performance: their perception of the other side's concerns. The villain of the piece is blurry vision by the light of hope, as each side looked abroad to gauge the other's bind and bite. These men made few mistakes when they took note of what the other side was *doing*. Perception of its actual behavior was not the problem. Comprehension of what lay behind behavior was the problem. There they made innumerable mistakes.

They did so because they repeatedly projected onto the other side two things stamped "made at home": an outcome which would suit their own convenience, and a series of alleged constraints sufficient to induce it. The other side's concerns were read accordingly.

The critical mistake in such a reading ran to their perception of the other side's constraints. For the alleged constraints seem powerfully to have reinforced considerations of convenience. Had Dulles known the British were unlikely to be hobbled by internal opposition, the sheer inconvenience of another outcome probably would not have been enough to keep him hopeful. Had Eden known that Eisenhower probably would want to dissociate Americans emphatically from allied intervention, he might not have been content to leave him in that posture for a week. Had Macmillan known how critical for Kennedy were budgetary tactics, he might not have waited on events. Had McNamara known that Thorneycroft was sitting still he almost certainly would have bestirred himself. In all such instances, a faulty reading of the other side lent these men confidence that its behavior would match their convenience. Otherwise, despite the inconvenience, they might well have taken thought about their chosen course: back to the drawing board.

Whence came these misperceptions of the other side's constraints? Sometimes they came from false analogies with past occasions on the other side as those had been enshrined, usually incorrectly, in one's own beliefs—thus, for example, Whitehall's view of Truman's Jewish vote analogized to Eisenhower's forthcoming election. Washington's view of Whitehall's clever chaps is probably in the same class, a false analogy from men who had been young in World War II and thrilled by Winston Churchill at a distance. Sometimes the misperceptions came from false analogies with past occasions of one's own, which would constrain if the positions were reversed. In the back of Eden's mind, reportedly, as he considered Ike-the-doggo, was a British General Election, where government stops stock-still. Evidently in the front of McNamara's mind lay the presumption that his counterpart-by-title was his counterpart in function.

Either way, these men dredged their perceptions of the other side's constraints out of their own heads. They reasoned by analogy and drew conclusions for the other side, and thereupon perceived what they projected. In this there is an interesting tautology: perceptions reinforced their own convenience which had led them in the first place toward selection of analogies on which to base perceptions. Thus they drew aid and comfort in proceeding on their own side to do what they felt they had to do within their own constraints. Thereby they set the stage for their own disappointment and its aftermath in paranoid reactions.

Projection of constraints, reasoning by analogy, compensates a busy man for unfamiliarity in an uncertain world. Someone else's government machine is something of a mystery. What may emerge from it by way of future action cannot help but be a speculative matter in advance. It thus save time and trouble to analogize; it also short-cuts arguments which by their nature cannot be pre-tested. And to select analogies that reinforce one's own convenience is to do no more than keep one's eye on one's own business. The impulse is as natural as breathing to a man who has to manage by and through his own machine. Of this I shall have more to say in Chapter VI.

Necessitous relations inside governments, productive of behavior in these terms, go far to help us characterize the hazards in relations between friends like Washington and London, but not far enough. We have seen this behavior lead to crisis, straining relations hard. But if behavior of this sort is rooted in such natural responses as I now suggest, why are there not hard strains upon

relations of all sorts and everywhere at once? Blurry
vision by the light of hope seems usual, not exceptional.
What makes it so pernicious in encounters between
Anglo-Saxon cousins?

Misperceiving others in this fashion is not confined to
situations of such close alliance. Leaving aside London
for the moment, there seem to be innumerable instances
in Washington's appraisals of estranged or hostile governments. During the early 1960s Americans had wishful thoughts aplenty of de Gaulle constrained by costs
in nuclear development as though he were a bourgeois
Finance Minister. During the later 1960s some of us, in
highest places, clung to thoughts of Ho Chi Minh constrained by "pain" as though he were a Senator hungry
for public works. And inside our own government the
tendency can be as marked when one department's bureaucrats size up another's. Between officials of Defense
and State, or Education and Justice, wishful elements
are often just as strong.

The same thing can be said of reticence, of stifled communication, which aggravated the misreadings in our
crisis by sustaining them. This too is a phenomenon
found in hostile relations as in friendly ones, and internally as well as internationally. The sievelike quality
of sovereignty, at least for us, is not the product only of
relationships among bureaucracies in an alliance. It also
is the product of news media and their pervasive links
with Washingtonians. In an age of instantaneous trans-
mission, it takes few words from a foreign source of
any stripe to let one part of Washington hear "prematurely" what another part has planned. We sometimes
can rely upon an adversary—especially if dictatorial—not

to let the "wrong" words slip at the "wrong" time to the "wrong" newsmen. But always this is risky, the more so with neutrals or friends, perhaps, than with acknowledged enemies. Although he may be spared collegial air forces or foreign offices, the prudent Washingtonian still finds reasons for reticence toward those with whom he deals, even as he ponders their constraints. Since reticence invites a like response, he thus adds to the prospect that if he has misperceived he will persist in doing so.

I speak just now of Washington and Washingtonians. With some adjustments of detail in cultural and institutional respects the same points seem to me to hold for London and for Londoners.

The crisis pattern with which I began this chapter contains elements found frequently in situations of noncrisis. Two strands of the pattern are pervasive in Anglo-American behavior: muddled perceptions and stifled communications. It follows that their corollary, the third strand, is commonplace: disappointed expectations. Yet relatively speaking, the fourth strand is a rarity. Paranoid reactions do not always or inevitably stem from disappointment. When they do, the stage is set for crisis.

IV

With one exception, men in our machine seem rarely to be shaken by the blighting of their hopes for outcomes in another machine. Witness our response when Soviet troops invade a satellite, or when Hanoi turns down another peace feeler (or witness the State Department's response when—as so often happens—our Treasury Department turns out to be conducting its own foreign policy). In instances of these sorts there is surely disappointment, but it does not seem to induce paranoia, or not for long; rather the result seems usually to be a relatively cool recalculation. As with Washington, so with London; the two appear substantially alike in this respect. Contrast the consequences in my crisis summaries. These speak to the exception: paranoid reactions are associated with relations bearing something like the burden of an unrequited love.

Misperceptions evidently make for crisis in proportion to the intimacy of relations. Hazards are proportionate to the degree of friendship. Indifference and hostility may not breed paranoia; friendship does.

In theory, friendship should provide a form of compensation: closeness spells acquaintance. If there is special risk in one friend's reading of another, there also is a special chance for accuracy. Both are fruits of friendship. Theoretically, these ought to cancel out. But evidently they do not.

In practice, as my crisis summaries suggest, acquaintance has wrapped up in it a faulty sense of competence, hence misplaced confidence. Instead of countering inaccuracy this contributes to it. Remember the cliche: "a little knowledge is a dangerous thing." So with acquaintance between friends, at least when they resemble Washington and London. For these, the two most intimate of peacetime allies known to modern history (excepting only Berlin and Vienna fifty years ago), acquaintance did not render misperception less. In the Suez case, still more in Skybolt, their knowledge rather aided and abetted their misreadings. It opened up to each side a rich storehouse of analogies and hid from sight uncertainties attendant on their use. All too seldom did the men on either side address the question: if we do harm to others in their terms what could they do to us in ours? That is the classic question asked of adversaries. It focuses attention on the other's terms and hedges confident analogizing. In the instances before us, "they," alas, were "friends."

Throughout these crises signs abound that close acquaintance was more burdensome than beneficial, more conducive to misreading then to accurate perception. Consider the degree to which chief officers of government on either side took their own word for what constrained the other side, played their own hunches, drew their own conclusions. Acquaintance ran so deep that each American conceived himself an expert on the British, and *vice versa*. Such are the consequences of a common language, a shared history, wartime collaboration, intermarriage, all abetted by air travel and the telephone. But confidence in one's own expertise diminishes one's sense of need to probe, reduces one's incentive to ask questions, removes from sight the specialists of whom these might be asked, and also pushes out of sight the usefulness of feedback. Recall what happened in the critical pre-public stages of these crises to that "private wire," the secure telephone, linking chiefs of government in Washington and London. It went unused. This serves us as a symbol for the burdensome effects of close acquaintance.

Still, I would guess that these Americans and Englishmen knew more of one another than the specialists in their regimes could claim to know about most of their counterparts in other major governments. A little knowledge may be dangerous, but, relatively speaking, these self-constituted experts knew a lot. Yet we have seen how frequently they read each other wrong, how often their perceptions were inaccurate enough to risk the very things they sought from one another and to store in their own heads the stuff of paranoid reactions, hazarding a breach in their relations.

This raises an insistent question: should these men have been able to do better than they did? Granting them their troubles but considering their resources, should they not have been capable of less misunderstanding?

The question goes to the heart of the alliance task these men confronted. Each worked from his own side of the alliance to shape outcomes stemming from the other side. When one side seeks to influence the conduct of another, everything depends upon the accuracy with which those who would wield influence perceive constraints impinging on the other side's behavior (and apply what they perceive in their own actions). As between London and Washington, you may think this an easy task, the easier for ties of language and the like. If so, my cast of characters will seem a foolish lot. Far from it; they were mostly men of high intelligence and wide experience. Each acted reasonably within his own constraints. Each failed to grasp some aspect of a foreigner's constraints. But this too becomes reasonable in the degree to which it actually was foreign. The difficulty of their task cannot be unrelated to the subtleties of difference they encountered in the inner workings of their governments. A judgment of their capability to do better depends in part upon a judgment of those subtleties as sources for misunderstanding.

Having posed the question, let me now defer an answer. Before you can assess their handling of the task you need to see the things that tripped them up. Therefore, suspend your judgment of these men while we take time to look inside their governments. Then you will be better able to make judgments.

V: London and Washington

"LONDON" and "Washington" are shorthand terms for vast machines of government, which labeled "A" and "B" we would be less likely to personify. These are not "friendly" in the sense of human individuals, nor is my inquiry addressed to human friendship. We deal here with the friendship of machines. Before I turn to differences in their internal workings, let me give you a quick sketch of the working parts. Then you can more readily observe the shades of difference, part by part.

I

These machines are not manlike, although men are in them. Each machine is a complex array of mutually dependent, institutionalized "positions." These are known to us as public offices, elective or appointive as the case may be. Each position is linked to many others along lines of set procedure for getting things done. These procedural lines are known to us by such catch phrases as budgetary process, legislative programming, nominating process, cable traffic. However known, these lines are "action channels," regularized means of moving to decision, taking action or avoiding it.

Each position and each channel has a history, reflecting a succession of laws, customs, precedents, and past incumbents. These frame the work requirements for every new incumbent.

In each position sits a man discharging it as best he can in light of its requirements and his ambitions as he sees them—brains and temperament allowing—in short, by his totality of human "interests." That totality emphatically includes his sense of duty, and loyalties: personal, political, programmatic. He is no *homo economicus*.

For action purposes, each man is linked to many other men, although in no sense equally to all, by the procedural channels running past or through their jobs as well as his. Precisely how their work relates to his for given purposes defines the link in given situations. Our Secretaries of State and Treasury, for instance, are linked differently when diplomatic action calls for words as against money.

A man may have another link to colleagues. Depending on procedures for selection and advancement, his future may be governed by their judgment—shades of Anthony Eden.

For want of better words, the moves toward action in a government machine—from positions, through channels—can be termed a "game," the men becoming "players." The game they play is known as governing their country. Their object is public authority wielded (or withheld) for substantive purposes. They play for "stakes" deriving from their interests. It is sometimes fun but not a sport; nor on the evidence before you do they take it so. I urge you not to do so either.

A player's stakes blend personal with substantive con-

cerns. For every player, any move toward action brings
an element of personal challenge wrapped in a substantive guise. Of these his stakes are made. The substance
is important, never doubt it, for that is what the game is
all about. But so is the personal element. It makes no
difference whether the move is of his own making or
arises from sources outside his control. Either way, involvement of his job in some degree involves himself.
Attached to his position are assorted expectations in the
minds of his associates, evoked by its requirements and
his career. Attached to his position also are his expectations of himself. Both sorts of expectations are reflected
in his interests. He is man-in-office, with a record to defend and a future to advance, not least in history. The
personal is tightly interwoven with the institutional. It
is a rare player who can keep the two distinct, much
less view both apart from substance. None was so rare in
the cases before you.

Accordingly, this is a game in which the stakes rise
high. Whether they are high or low for any given player
depends upon the expectations centering on him. These
can change as rapidly as the surrounding circumstances
alter in the eyes of other players. Hence the stakes are
subject to quick change. Stakes can be far lower than
were Dulles's when he withdrew our offer on Aswan.
Stakes can rise as fast as his did at the moment the Canal
was seized "because" of that withdrawal. And stakes can
rise as high as Eden's on the eve of intervention. In public life, there is nothing higher than that: the prize of
office and the fruits of policy, along with the verdict of
history. What matters more to a man than his head when
he identifies it with the public good?

The working parts as here described are common to both Washington and London. Moreover these machines, the British and American, have common origins: the British Constitution and English common law. They also share the hallmarks of "democracy," as understood on our side of the globe. Both governments are constitutional in character, representative in form, limited in scope, confined by guarantees of private right, hence private property, and legitimatized by the symbols of popular sovereignty. Finally, they share a working language (more or less), a source of endless trouble in their dealings with each other.

Accordingly, the game of governance as played in both machines is broadly speaking the same game. Action channels and positions in the one bear a family resemblance to those in the other. But resemblance is deceptive. Only in an overview are these machines alike. Only in the broad are their games the same. Details diverge. The players in our cases ran afoul of the details.

Every schoolboy and most statesmen on both sides can catalogue gross differences: presidential versus cabinet government, federalism versus centralism, factionalism versus party discipline, a written Constitution versus parliamentary self-restraint, all in the context of a newly populated continent versus a long-settled island. But these were known to everyone in 1956 and 1962 as well as now. Why then the misperceptions of our crises?

Misperceptions in these crises were occasioned not by the gross differences but rather by small shadings—sometimes hidden, often subtle—in their application to positions and to channels, thus to players and to stakes of human interest. We were tripped up by nuances.

As between London and Washington the differences that count lurk at this lower level of nuance, of fine detail.

II

What are the "little" differences between these two machines? Or rather, more precisely, what were they in the time span of our crises? Both machines evolve and change with time. Answers for the middle Fifties and the early Sixties will be wrong, to some degree, a decade hence. Still, we learn a lot by looking at the past decade. As of then, what were the nuances?

By way of answer, let us move back through our crises, taking note of things these players stumbled over when they looked across the water at each other. Thus we can at once uncover differences and register the difficulties of these men. I offer you a dozen instances, subsumed under four categories. These are broad categories, by no means mutually exclusive, and meant to be suggestive, not definitive. They help, however, to illuminate small differences. I think that you will find them much more useful for the purpose than formal institutional divisions.

The first category is political accountability; it deals with stakes of players stemming from the press of party politics on their positions. This is a heavy weight in topmost places, British and American alike. The second category is SOPs, standard operating procedures; it deals with stakes of players stemming from the twists and turns in action channels as these flow through, or around, their positions. Relative relationships to given channels confer relative advantages on men in jobs. The third category is job-to-job relationships; it deals with stakes of players stemming from the links between their own positions and assorted others as personified in given individuals. The fourth category is on-the-job perspectives; it deals with stakes of players stemming from the substance in a governmental action seen—as they are bound to see— by light of their positions. This, of course, is light strained through the fixed ideas they may have brought to office from their schooling and experience.

My stress is upon *stakes*. For this there is good reason. As we have seen, paranoid behavior follows misperceived constraints. At every turning point in Suez and in Skybolt, constraints were but the passive voice of stakes.

Looking for shades of difference in our two machines, we begin with political accountability. Consider two instances, one British, one American, both taken from the Suez story.

First, in September and October 1956, Dulles and his President seem to have drawn much comfort from the rising press and parliamentary opposition Eden was encountering at home. This they counted on to reinforce their own foot-dragging against British intervention by armed force. I have suggested that our men may have analogized to their experience in 1954 when Democratic leaders in Congress stood against our intervention at the time of Dien Bien Phu. If so, the analogy was faulty.

In modern British practice, a Prime Minister whose party has a good working majority in Commons, as Eden's did, need heed the Opposition party and the press only if and as their views are strongly shared in Cabinet and his own back benches. Cabinet dissension means much; especially in context of back-bench dissension.

But opposition from the Opposition counts next to nothing. For Eisenhower during 1954, plagued by McCarthyites and Brickerites in Republican ranks, the Minority Leader of the Senate, Lyndon Johnson, was a power to be reckoned with—also a helping hand. Not so Hugh Gaitskell in the reckoning of Eden.

Americans have been brought up on Bagehot, read at first or second hand, which is a pity. For *The English Constitution* shows us Westminster and Whitehall of the 1860s, a time when party discipline was relatively lax, when Independent Members lived up to the name, when Governments were actually dependent upon changeable majorities in Common. Ninety years later all was different.

Nowadays when lines are drawn in Commons for and against the Government, its MPs rarely nerve themselves to vote in dangerous numbers against their own front bench. For if they are ambitious they can have no place to go except toward that bench themselves; no one can help them get there save the men who sit there. And if they find contentment in remaining where they are, their safest course is to appear consistent, which usually means following their leaders. Those who nominate MPs seem to admire that; so, apparently, do most constituents.

In the days of Eden's premiership—also Macmillan's for the Skybolt case—Tories held a comfortable majority of seats in Common. No Minister was worried about losing votes of confidence. No one thought the Opposition capable of drawing a majority out of desertions from Conservative ranks. That sort of thing occurred only in textbooks. By all accounts available to me, what worried modern Ministers was not desertions but abstentions.

The Tories had been traumatized in 1940 when abstentions on their own side yielded Neville Chamberlain so relatively narrow a majority as to impair beyond recall the public image of his Government. He went. By this route Tory Premiers ever since have feared to go.

Yet in 1956, so far as back-bench sentiment among Conservatives was organized against the Government, it was to Eden's right, not to his left, hard line not soft line, centered in the "Suez Group," so-called, which had emerged two years before out of antipathy to the Egyptian course that he, as Foreign Secretary, had set for Churchill's Government.

Eisenhower and Dulles were correct in thinking Suez posed a parliamentary threat to Eden's premiership. But it was the sort of threat to spur him on, not slow him down. So, I think, it did.

Second, at the outset of October 1956, when Macmillan came from Washington with word of Eisenhower "doggo until election," this fed what I understand to have been Eden's preconception—widely shared within his Foreign Office—that the New York Jewish vote was a trump card. The proffered French-Israeli deal thus offered Eden more than his desired contingency. It also seemed to promise our passivity in the event. This reasoning Macmillan evidently also shared; his word, at any rate, set off the forward march. The Cabinet assented to the deal immediately after his return.

The preconception in this instance stemmed, as I have noted, from Foreign Office observation of a President eight years before, when Truman had reversed his State Department, overruling the revered George Catlett Marshall, to announce immediate recognition for the State of

Israel. Truman himself stoutly denies party-political motivations for this act. Knowing Truman I am quite prepared to think he may be right. But Londoners were not alone in drawing opposite conclusions. Every wise-acre in Washington had heard accounts of Secretary Marshall's snub to the then White House Counsel, Clark M. Clifford, who supposedly was told: "If it weren't for domestic politics you'd have no part in this matter."

However that may be, the politics of 1948 were a far cry from those of 1956. Especially was this the case in White House perspective. For Truman the Democrat, heir to Roosevelt's coalition yet threatened by defection from its left—from Henry Wallace—the loyalties of accustomed Democrats in New York City, Jews among them, were prospectively a key to the election. Actually, Truman lost the state and still won his election, but this outcome seemed unlikely in advance. Whereas for Eisenhower the Republican, whose party rarely had been more united, the loyalties of downstate New Yorkers counted less. Republican majorities were built upstate, not down. Besides, as National Hero, which he genuinely was, he always seemed assured of re-election.

Eisenhower evidently wanted to win big. Here indeed, New Yorkers of all sorts were relevant. He wanted for himself the largest possible majority of votes, and for his party a majority of seats in Congress. The two were thought to be related. Eisenhower's "coattails" were the means by which his party hoped to win control of Congress. By this reckoning, a Jewish vote might serve as well as anybody else's, but no better, and a stance for "peace" pleased all.

The British view of Truman's reckoning in 1948
appears almost irrelevant for 1956, but easy to apply,
hence tempting. The British calculation turned upon
American electoral arithmetic. We give our Presidency
to the candidate with popular pluralities in enough
states to produce a majority in the Electoral College.
There, with rare exceptions, every state's Electors vote
alike, according to the popular plurality at home. Each
state has a number of electors roughly in proportion to
its share of the national population. New York Electors
constituted almost ten per cent of the whole College.
The narrowest of popular pluralities sufficed to win
them all. And Jews were thought to constitute a fifth of
New York voters. If Eisenhower were to punish Israel
before election might they not vote en bloc to punish
him? Might that not then cost him New York's Electors?

If this is what the British saw, their calculation missed
three points. First it missed the point that many of those
voters would be faithful to the Democrats in any case.
Not even Eisenhower's big win, much less a bare plurality, required that they swing to him *en masse*. It also
missed the point that New York was dispensable for
him, except symbolically—and congressionally—in terms
of that big win. The Electoral College would be his
regardless. That was as certain as such things can be.
And still a further point was missed: should Eisenhower
fear to harm Israelis, his fear would vanish with the
need once Israel had beaten the Egyptians. Eden's hold
on Jewish voters did not match Ben-Gurion's. If Eisenhower were to stay his hand on their account why would
he do so one day longer than he had to?

In the event, perhaps coincidentally, we did not harm

Israel, which had achieved its own objectives by the time
an adverse action at the UN reached a vote. Initially
we acted only in that quarter, with our call for a cease-
fire. This gave the Israelis six days. They wanted more
time, mostly as a courtesy to their allies who had assured
them victory by holding over Egypt's head the prospect
of a second front. We let two more days pass without
demur except on paper. By the night before Election
Day, when Humphrey threatened London, there was
no one left to harm save our allies.

Our turn to the UN sounded the theme of disassoci-
ation. It reassured Americans on "peace," at least for
us. But Eisenhower had become so angry at the war-
makers that his reported impulse was to seek a UN resolution branding them "aggressors." On the Korean
precedent this would have seemed a call for forceful
intervention to restore the territorial integrity of Egypt.
Dulles not surprisingly seems to have stood with Eisenhower. I am told that it was Harold Stassen, the then
White House disarmament adviser, who talked them
into relative passivity, "cease-fire." Reportedly what
preyed on Stassen's mind was Moscow. Conceivably he
may have had some voters on his mind as well. He often
did. But he is said to have confined his argument to foreign policy.

In a way, Ike did indeed lie doggo until the very eve
of our election. He did so partly on account of Hungary,
it seems, which no one had expected when Macmillan
brought his cheery word to Cabinet. The doing did not
keep us out of the UN. This upset Eden greatly, and
Lloyd no less. It made them wield their veto in the

Security Council, Moscow-style, a jarring thing to English sensibilities. But we forebore to brand them aggressors, which would have been more jarring still. Nor did we interfere with allied operations. Our Mediterranean Fleet may have been poised to do so, yet did not.

What more could Eden have expected? Apparently he had conceived that we would spare his feelings too, and give him up to fourteen days, not eight. If so, he had a strange view of our voters and our voting—and of Eisenhower.

However, what seems strange to us in our terms may have seemed more usual to him in his. I have a strong impression that on his side of the water, front-bench politicians of the time could give party-political concerns free play in foreign policy—to say nothing of economic policy—with a straightforward consciousness quite inadmissable, indeed almost unthinkable, for Presidents on our side.

We proceeded then in an inhibiting framework of "bipartisanship" built by FDR and Truman—and maintained by Eisenhower after his own fashion—to afford support for a revolution in our foreign relations, breaching the isolationist tradition. Men who had been bred in that tradition before shifting ground themselves, now sought to keep the country with them on the plea that "politics stops at the water's edge." This, for them, could not be a mere slogan. For them it was a virtual imperative of personal conduct. Truman tried to live by it and rarely let his conscious mind admit inevitable lapses. Eisenhower seems to have done the same, not least when he embarked upon that UN resolution.

Conservatives in Britain knew a different imperative: above all, Tories ought to govern. Perhaps Eden mistook Eisenhower for a Tory.

On a superficial view of our electoral system such a one might have performed as Eden wanted, overcompensating to assure a big win in New York. I grant you that to render this believable the view must be extremely superficial. So Eden's seems to have been. In fairness let me add that he does not seem to have based his expectations on New York alone. Reportedly he had another basis, no less superficial, turning not on party politics but on defense: our stake in Panama. To this I will return.

III

Turning from nuances in political accountability we come to my second category, operating procedures. What shades of difference here are illustrated by our crises? Let me give you three instances, two British, one American, drawn from Skybolt and Suez combined.

First, early in November 1962, Kennedy and his associates agreed that since our Skybolt cancellation would create a British problem, London should be warned in time to seize it, to resolve it, and to tell us what was wanted. Our men conceived correctly that the problem was important, running to the heart of British defense policy and also to the heart of party politics: the independent nuclear deterrent. We also thought the Tories had a firm hold on their own machine, with Commons in the pocket of the Cabinet. Macmillan and his colleagues, being clever chaps, would know a thorny

problem when they saw it, and would grasp it. In this
we made an error opposite to Dulles's concerning Parliament. We did not overrate the Opposition or back
benchers, but we underrated the collegiality of the front
bench. We misread the inner character of Cabinet procedure.

London was proceeding with a "Government Decision," an official Cabinet action, taken two years earlier.
This constituted a commitment to the independent
nuclear deterrent, premised on the Camp David Agreement for Skybolt. Macmillan's heart was set on the
deterrent. That two-year-old decision assured it to him.
Cabinet action committed permanent officials, civil and
military alike. It also committed the Conservative majority in Commons. His deterrent was safe at least until
the next General Election; and no doubt he meant to
make it an election issue. Washington's warning put
this whole structure in doubt. Our warning posed an
"iffy" question. To raise it with his colleague was to risk
their commitment. Any substitute for Skybolt on its
present terms would cost *new* money, funds not previously earmarked. Whence was it to come? From social
services? Or aircraft carriers? Besides, Polaris in particular was hated by the Air Force and unwanted by
the Navy. Faced thus might the Cabinet undo its decision? The Prime Minister wanted none of that.

Reportedly, Macmillan never let the "iffy" question
near his Cabinet. Sensible Prime Ministers do not take
such things there. Instead he acted as though Britain
had no problem, as though what was "iffy" ran the other
way, a matter of our honor not his need: would Kennedy
repudiate an Eisenhower agreement? In short, Mac-

millan stood upon the status quo, and clung to it
determinedly until he got to Nassau in December. Then,
when he was forced to shift his ground and managed
to make good with the Americans, he put before the
Cabinet his Polaris deal by cable, asking prompt response
since Kennedy was waiting. His Foreign and Defence
Secretaries were with him when he cabled. The Cabinet
acceded, cost and Service anguish notwithstanding. What
else could they have done?

As for Macmillan's Defence Secretary, Thorneycroft,
the man to whom our warning was addressed, when he
received it he had reasons of his own for keeping just
as quiet as his Prime Minister. He too was wedded to
a nuclear deterrent. He may well have preferred Polaris
to Skybolt. But our warning gave him no option to say
so: advocacy in advance of cancellation from our side—
accompanied by a compensatory offer—would make him
seem a traitor to his Air Force and Macmillan. While
Thorneycroft waited for our cancellation he apparently
said nothing in his Ministry. When we made no compensatory offer, he embraced the status quo and bran-
dished it in public against us.

Our men conceived their warning as a means to mo-
bilize the British. It had an opposite effect. Immobility
resulted. The reasons are not far to seek. They go to the
heart of government by colleagues.

The Cabinet governs through assertion of two strong
conventions. One I mentioned earlier: its hold upon
MPs. The other is its hold on permanent officials, who
will do as they are told provided that the telling comes
in proper form from their own Minister (within his
jurisdiction) or from Cabinet, as the last stage of com-

mittee work in which they have engaged. While effectively asserted, these conventions offer Cabinet members
an unlimited power. But by definition it adheres to
them collectively. Agreement or at least show of solidarity is needed to induce it. Nothing risks back-bench
acquiescence more than front-bench disarray. Nothing
risks bureaucratic acquiescence more than a failure of
form. For those two conventions are in essence tacit
treaties. MPs surrender judgment to a leadership committee in return for governance reflective of their interests, political and other; hence the stress on solidarity.
Bureaucrats exchange obedience for consultation, for
assurance of a hearing; hence the stress on form.

As instruments of power, British Cabinets approxi-
mate our Presidency and Congress combined, along with
heads of federal agencies, state governors and legisla-
tures, mayors of major cities, and the Supreme Court.
Besides, front benches are informally the counterparts
of presidential nominating conventions. Yet for this very
reason the exercise of power is a sticky business, as sticky
to Englishmen as to Americans. Where we have public
struggles by avowedly independent institutions, they
have private struggles by ostensibly united Ministries
and Ministers. Very frequently our struggles approach
stalemate. So do theirs. But unlike us they need to keep
such things from public sight, lest solidarity and form
be compromised. This inhibition makes their system all
the stickier.

In Cabinet, changing course is hard, and hazardous.
To quote the private comment of a very close observer:
"The obverse of our show of monolithic unity behind a
Government position when we have one is slowness,

ponderousness, deviousness, in approaching a position, getting it taken, getting a 'sense of the meeting.' Nothing in our system is harder to do, especially if press leaks are at risk."

Those who would innovate proceed at risk. Timing has inordinate importance. Especially is this the case for a Prime Minister who knows his mind but is uncertain of his colleagues. For the ranks of bureaucrats are theirs, not his. Officials serve departments headed by his colleagues. And the loyalties of back benchers do not run to him alone. He has to take his colleagues into camp before he can command their troops. Should he remain uncertain he is well advised to wait, and meanwhile steer the settled course. Macmillan waited. This was not hard to do: one thing a PM can control himself is the Cabinet agenda.

Second, the same procedural constraints lay back of a misreading from our side during the Suez crisis. Another Prime Minister who knew his mind was Eden after Egypt seized the Canal. Far from waiting he then rounded up his colleagues, voiced their common shock, enhanced their anger by his own, and gained assent to a contingent use of force. That assent gave him the leeway to prepare for the contingency. He did so in selective consultation with a shifting set of colleagues and a narrow band of permanent officials, mostly military. His secretiveness increased as Dulles's initiative—and Nasser's prudence—made the contingency harder to reach.

Thereby Eden skated on thin ice, right to the edges both of solidarity and of form. The record does not show that he slipped over either edge. The colleagues whose portfolios or party standing gave them "need to know" were kept sufficiently informed so none could claim he lacked a voice. The senior permanent official in the Foreign Office, also the Cabinet Secretary, and of course the Chiefs of Staff, were in the know. Every other departmental civil servant was excluded. This cost Eden dear when his finances struck a snag they could have spotted in advance. But keeping them in ignorance was well within his rights, so long as their masters—his colleagues—concurred, which they did.

Yet despite its very different look, Eden's conduct speaks to the same order of constraints as does Macmillan's six years later. A governmental course was set by the initial Cabinet action, Eden in the van. Were it to be reversed he must again be in the van; he scarcely could afford "repudiation." But neither could he afford to show "weakness." Besides, he *wanted* use of force. He wanted it so much that he embraced Franco-Israeli plans. Rejection for the sake of "honor" might have given him safe grounds on which to seek reversal from his colleagues: rather spare Wogs than connive with Frogs (to say nothing of Israelis). Who could have thought this weakness? Instead he chose to help those planners manufacture a contingency in substitution for the ones Egyptian caution and our strictures were removing from sight. Then, at another moment of collegial anger, this time against Dulles, he sought Cabinet assent to switch contingencies. He got it. With it he gained cover for all subsequent secretive undertakings.

Eden managed to make Cabinet power serve his purpose, but the very way he did it left him vulnerable when his use of force, once under way, encountered our man Humphrey. At the crucial Cabinet meeting where our "ultimatum" was discussed, its nature left no room for failing to consult the Treasury and none for failing to respect the Chiefs of Staff. The latter judged—quite wrongly, it appears—that five or six more days were needed to complete their operation. Chancellor Macmillan, briefed at last by his officials, judged the pound could not survive that long without help from the IMF, where Humphrey had a veto. Caught between the two, Eden cracked.

Evidently this astonished Dulles, judging by his alleged remark to Britain's Foreign Secretary Selwyn Lloyd: "Why did you stop?" In light of the estimates of field commanders at the time and commentators since, that question echoes down the years. It seems two days at most, not five or six, could have sufficed to secure the Canal, and in these days Macmillan could have been at Humphrey constantly, or Eden at Eisenhower, promising and warning. Meanwhile, even a hint of Humphrey's threat could have served to keep officials in line, also Tories, to say nothing of men-on-the-streets: anti-Americanism would have been a tonic.

Yet Eden's vulnerability at this juncture—health aside —shows how thin was the ice on which he previously had skated. His colleagues had assented to the use of force, but not to consequences such as these, and their assent had been obtained by means which left most of them uncommitted in detail, hence free to disengage. The scheme was his and Lloyd's, not theirs; so were the plots and plans. This had made it easier to gain their acquiescence. Now it made it harder to keep them up to scratch. Macmillan, once so keen for force, could now reverse himself on departmental grounds with no embarrassment.

The Chiefs of Staff, meanwhile, had planned the war according to their lights, and now were executing it according to their fashion. Civilian meddling in the Cabinet's name they had to tolerate, but not meddling from the PM alone. They served the Queen, which is to say the Government, not him; and "she" was scarcely proof against the possibility that if pushed very hard they might resign. This was no Government of National Coalition but a Tory Cabinet with a war contested by the Opposition. Eden's colleagues had no stomach for a contest also with their military advisers. This logic had sufficed to keep the seaborne landings sacrosanct in Musketeer. Now it sufficed again. The Chiefs of Staff presumably were only doing what professionals so placed will often do: padding numbers in the search for a safe answer. Never mind.

Eden could not make the Chiefs assure him a quick finish. At most he might have asked them for another estimate, while calling on the Chancellor for still another day. But if Macmillan refused it, as apparently he did, and if most other seniors fell away, what then? Then only by a show of will which mesmerized his colleagues, casting all the fear of party-gods into them, could Eden have gone on. Some men might have accomplished that. Not Eden. He had used up the advantages of office. He also had used up himself. Physically and emotionally he was drained. His plight speaks to the exercise of power inside a collegium.

An American Administration is a collegial body of a sort and in a way, but certainly not of this sort, nor precisely in this way. Behind the Dulles inquiry "Why did you stop?" lie procedures of a presidential system where one man's word suffices, at the least, to buy a few days' time from his subordinates. Eden, *in extremis*, lacked subordinates; he had Colleagues.

Still, our President confronts procedural constraints of other sorts which can be almost equally compelling. These are no better understood by Englishmen than Cabinet conventions are by us. By way of illustration, here is a third instance, this one drawn from Skybolt.

In November 1962, Macmillan, then Prime Minister, waited on events with confidence, apparently, that President Kennedy was under no compulsion to upset the status quo. Our Chiefs of Staff were known to favor Skybolt. There was no outcry against it in Congress or the press. No doubt its development was costly, far exceeding estimates, but this had happened on both sides of the Atlantic with new weapons ever since the war. Besides, the Americans knew as well as he that British entry to the Common Market now hung in the balance and that this was not a time to trouble other waters: they wanted Britain in the EEC as much as he did, if not more.

Why then would we insist on making trouble? Macmillan evidently saw no reason unless Kennedy were out to do him harm. This, I am told, he discounted.

Such reasoning was logical except in one particular. It left out of account our budgetary process. For Kennedy was under a compulsion, or at least a strong temptation, created by the politics of American-style budgeting.

As I already have mentioned, the Kennedy Administration stood to save $2.5 billion in three years, provided

Skybolt could be stopped once and for all. But presidential wishes would not guarantee the saving. Congress must acquiesce. The weapon had good friends there: key committee members in both Houses who owed no thanks to the President for their seniority. How best to curb their friendship? By way of answer McNamara invoked a standard tactic which he probably regretted not having employed the year before on the B-70. This tactic was to take the weapon out of Kennedy's next Annual Budget, which in any case was sure to show a deficit. If Skybolt's friends then sought congressional action to finance it, the onus of "new" cost would fall on them in context of that deficit.

Annual Budgets go to Congress in January. Were Skybolt to be kept out of the next one, it must be cancelled by December. If it remained in being it would have to be budgeted. The President would then have lost his chance to shift the onus. For the Annual Budget was *his* presentation. Skybolt's presence there would carry his endorsement, which its friends could cite against a later cancellation. To deny them that advantage he must cancel now. Otherwise they might succeed in financing the weapon for another fiscal year. By then sunk costs would be so high that friends could make a most compelling case for its completion and production. In prospect there went the whole $2.5 billion. Kennedy could best belie that prospect by immediate cancellation. So McNamara evidently told him. The argument apparently convinced not only Kennedy but also Rusk, the Secretary of State.

Actually, there might have been a way at once to defer cancellation and to guarantee the saving. A President can "impound" funds voted by Congress and refuse to spend them. McNamara surely knew of this device. Indeed he had just used it to deny the Air Force funds appropriated despite him for the B-70. But for that very reason he reportedly did not wish to employ it soon again against the Air Force, especially not in context of embarrassment for Britain. Evidently neither did Kennedy.

To London all of this was quite incomprehensible. There are no close counterparts in British practice. Even the terms mean different things. There, Treasury officials oversee the spending of departments, and Department Heads appeal against the Chancellor in Cabinet. The outcome is definitive. A British Budget is not even couched in spending terms. What Parliament receives and votes under that label are measures to raise revenue, covering the Cabinet's expenditure decisions. Kennedy's particular temptation literally could not arise. If a Prime Minister were comparably tempted, his tactics would be set by Cabinet tempers, not by Parliamentary timetables.

Moreover, no Prime Minister had yet encountered McNamara's stakes in "cost effectiveness," or had been exposed to comparable analyses at home. The notion that a weapons system should be dropped because some abstruse calculation showed its whole cost relative to benefit, in dollar terms, higher than that of a presumptive substitute was quite as strange to English politicians of the time as to our Military Services. McNamara sought to teach our Services a lesson, which no doubt enhanced his interest in the Skybolt cancellation. But London could not know this, for his methods were not practiced there. The warning he conveyed there fit into no context of experience.

Six years earlier, I think the British stumbled over something rather comparable, but I also think they never knew it. In September and October 1956, they fumed at Dulles's refusal to assure Ex-Im Bank credits for the boycott they had read into his SCUA scheme. They seem not to have noticed that precisely at that time our Secretary of the Treasury had started what became a famous war against White House and Budget Bureau staff work on the January Budget. This is the war he subsequently lost in private, then made public. I have told that story elsewhere.[19] But even in October Humphrey's warfare was not altogether private. Early that month, in a major Detroit speech, he signaled the main lines of the attack he then was mounting against Eisenhower's budgeteers. Humphrey sent a copy of his speech to Dulles, noting "Here's the story on tight money. Feel free to lift from it."[20] Dulles did not do so. As far as I can find, he steadily forebore to join that fight on either side. It never was his way to expend energy where his position left him weak. But I believe he watched his step with special care that Fall when money was at stake, especially funds under Treasury control like those the British sought to have us pledge. If so, here is another instance of constraint attendant on procedure, in this case, again, our budgeting.

IV

Let me turn now from these matters of procedure to a closely connected category for distinguishing small differences between London and Washington. This is the category of job-to-job relations. We deal here with re-

lations among players whose positions are linked—of
necessity, not choice—by action channels or promotion
systems. Dulles and Humphrey are, of course, a case in
point. But more illuminating, I believe, are several
other instances. I offer you four, two British, two American, again drawn from both crises.

The first of these instances concerns Macmillan as
Chancellor of the Exchequer, in relation to Eden as
Prime Minister. In late September 1956, before Macmillan came home to report Ike's doggishness, he had
spent time in Washington. This lent credence to his
word. He had been there as Chancellor on Treasury
business, a meeting of the IMF, which brought him into
contact with his opposite number, Humphrey. Macmillan also saw Dulles at least once and paid a courtesy
call on his friend in the White House. Humphrey then
was only on the fringes of our Suez policy. Dulles and
Eisenhower, on the other hand, were in the midst of it.
They were its architects. Yet, after seeing them, Macmillan left there with those doggish notions firmly in
his head. How could they have allowed him to depart
in such a fashion?

Presumably they did so because they did not perceive
him as the key to British conduct. They evidently saw
him as a Humphrey in reverse, the Cabinet money-man,
powerful of course, disposed to war—they knew that—
but not a man-in-charge. Lloyd and Eden, not Macmillan, were their opposite numbers. What they may
have told the Chancellor I do not know. What they
forebore to emphasize sufficiently is obvious.

Events would show that Eisenhower meant what he
previously had written London, namely that he must

dispute the use of force save as a last resort if Cairo ran
amok. Eden was arranging now for Tel Aviv to do so.
Eisenhower and Dulles, knowing nothing of this, could
not have told Macmillan that these two were not the
same. But what they could have done, presumably, was
convey their own fixity of purpose. This they plainly
failed to do.

Why so? Personalities perhaps afford a partial answer.
Eisenhower and Macmillan both were men of private
charm, and fond of one another. Imprecision is commonplace when such as these engage in casual conversation.
Yet these two often had done business with each other
in the past, no lack of clarity about it. Had the President
perceived the Chancellor as crucial to our case, they
might have talked more pointedly of Suez, less of politics,
than it appears they did. Presumably he did not see
him so.

As Chancellor, Macmillan did indeed become the
key we were to turn much later in the day, when
Humphrey's threat invoked his ministerial brief. But
in advance of events which brought us to that pass, his
Treasury position was the least of his importance. What
made Macmillan crucial while he visited in Washington
was rather his own standing among leaders of his party
as one of the two most likely to succeed to Eden's
Premiership, whenever Eden—not a well man—chose
or had to go. Macmillan's star just then was on the rise.
He long had seemed a trifle radical for Tory leadership,
but his hard line on Egypt pleased the Right. Beyond
this, Eden personally seems to have viewed Macmillan's
rival, R. A. Butler, as unworthy of promotion. Like
Churchill before him (and Macmillan after), Eden evi-

dently never forgave Butler for his faithfulness to Neville
Chamberlain in 1938: of such stuff Ministers were to be
made, but not Prime Ministers. When Eden went, he
would be the first to give the Queen advice on his successor. While these two remained foremost in the race
there could be little doubt how his advice would run.

The Chancellor who came to Cabinet fresh from
Washington thus had a special hold on the Prime Minister. It evidently was maintained. Even though Macmillan may have been the man, above all, whose defection at the last caused Eden to call off his war, when
the time came for him to go Macmillan did succeed
him. By all accounts the Queen then chose as Eden
wanted. And this suggests that had Macmillan come
from Washington in sober mood, cautious not ebullient,
Eden might have drawn back from his deal, or at least
viewed its timing implications with a care these evidently never got.

For an American, the mutual relations of Macmillan
and Eden—and Butler—hold the fascination of a mystery. We have no close counterparts. These men had
lived in intimacy, power intertwined, on one front bench
or other, governing or opposing, for almost a generation.
So they would go on until each was ennobled or de-
ceased. Not even senior Senators on our side have to
live so; each by his seniority acquires a committee which
becomes a piece of power all his own. As for our Cabinet
Members, these are like ships passing in the night:
cleared from different ports and headed toward oblivion.
So far as I can find, Eden and Macmillan did not relish
one another. Their relationship was less friendly than
systemic. So for their relations with "Rab" Butler, who

served each, in turn, as colleague and lieutenant without
ever lessening their grudge against him. Among Ministers on our side, such long-lived relations are almost
unthinkable because there hardly ever is occasion for
them. Grudges abound in Washington, but those who
hold them go their separate ways in four years or in
eight. And Presidents have neither need nor scope to
choose their own successors out of their own Cabinets.
If Eisenhower failed to see Macmillan as a key, this
scarcely is surprising.

My second instance concerns Dulles as Secretary of
State and Eisenhower as President. In 1956 it seems that
Eden stumbled over these same nuances by thinking, as
apparently he did, that Dulles was separable from Eisenhower. Recurrently throughout the Suez Crisis Eden
reportedly toyed with and drew comfort from—the
notion that while Dulles was a devil, Eisenhower was a
friend who could be drawn away from him. But this
ignored the relative positions of the two. Dulles was no
colleague, no front bencher, and he evidently knew it;
his power was reflective and he evidently knew that too.
Indeed, few Secretaries of States have ever been more
conscious of dependence on the President, and none has
been more careful of his White House credit.[21] For anyone familiar with their personal relations it would have
been inconceivable that during 1956, of all years, Dulles
might be playing his own game, not Eisenhower's. Yet
this, it seems, was Eden's notion.

A former Foreign Secretary who had dealt with
Cordell Hull should be forgiven for assuming that a
Secretary of State might not speak the President's mind.
(So should a man who had found Dulles and Eisenhower

not of the same mind as recently as Dien Bien Phu.) But Hull's status and Dulles's in 1956 were worlds apart, no matter that they held the same position. Hull had been so senior a congressional politician, and remained so much a symbol to his kind, that FDR, who found him an intractable lieutenant, could not fire him. So he ignored or undercut him while leaving him in place. This is not an unfamiliar pattern to the British; nor was it unfamiliar in our past when Secretaries of State were often major politicians, sometimes even rivals for their party's presidential nomination. Since Roosevelt's time, however, the pattern has become unusual with us. Even Truman, weak as he then was in his first term, dismissed James Byrnes for failing to be properly subordinate. Byrnes by then had compromised his own once-strong political base, which made it easier. And Byrnes was the last of the breed. Dulles became the third Secretary in a row to lack that sort of base. Worse, he had reached for it and failed in 1950, when he campaigned for the Senate from New York. His claim upon his party two years later was no more than an acknowledged expertise.

Eisenhower first appointed Dulles without knowing much of him except by reputation, and reportedly without much liking him. Dulles took the post intent on gaining presidential confidence. He hungered to be an effective Secretary, and he evidently saw no other way to go. Despite appearances, especially in retrospect, everything I know about their early years suggests that Dulles did not find it easy going. Temperamentally there seem to have been few affinities between them. Operationally, the President had ideas of his own, experience to boot, and an unmatched acquaintance among foreign statesmen, especially in Europe. As Eisenhower took hold of his job he came increasingly to do as other Presidents had done, picking and choosing among numbers of advisers of whom Dulles was but one. Dien Bien Phu affords us an example. There are others. This reached a peak, reportedly, in preparations for the Summit during 1955, where Eisenhower went on Eden's urging to the cheers of aides such as Nelson Rockefeller and Harold Stassen, but not Dulles. There the President assumed the working chairmanship of his own delegation in a burst of personal activity. Six weeks later he was stricken by a heart attack. Only after that attack did Dulles win his way into unrivaled eminence as "Mr. Foreign Policy." He did so by responding scrupulously to his ailing chief's enforced dependence on him.

Thereafter it appears that Dulles kept Eisenhower's confidence in the same way he had won it. During the entire Suez crisis, for example, he apparently cleared every move with Eisenhower in advance, emphatically including cancellation of the Aswan Dam, and also every phase of SCUA. As I read the record, Eisenhower was no "patsy" in this process. Far from it, he was laying down the law: *he* wanted "peace." Dulles strained to keep it. He had every reason to exert himself. For in his circumstances all the gains of presidential confidence, so recently acquired to his satisfaction, would be risked by warfare with his name on it, with blame, in Eisenhower's eyes, attached to him.

In an election year with a new term in prospect, the Secretary of State who hungers for a second term—as Dulles surely did—but has no claim upon it independent of performance, would be most unlikely to play any hand at all apart from or against the crucial judge of his performance. Dulles, it appears, was no exception. Rather, his behavior so confirms this proposition that I think he would have switched sides instantly, encouraged force, had Eden or Macmillan won a change of heart from Eisenhower. They made their choice for war without endeavoring to gain assent from him. They did not see in him the key to Dulles's foot-dragging.

The British evidently thought relations were reversed, with Dulles as a key to Eisenhower. Unable to turn that, they evidently hoped their wartime comradeship, together with his politics, gave them keys of their own to him marked "emergency use only." They made an emergency, and having done so found these keys breaking in their hands. I do not think that had they tried their friend Ike earlier they could have won him. Far from it; his opposition to their course was strongly grounded. I suggest no more than that for Suez purposes he really was President and they did not know it. In this they had a lot of company, both then and since. Dulles, however, was not of their number.

Now let me shift the scene from 1956 to 1962. My next two instances are drawn from Skybolt. These I shall treat together, since in many ways they are each other's mirror image. I refer on the one hand to McNamara as our Secretary of Defense in his relations with his President and Services, and with the State Department, and on the other hand to Thorneycroft as British Defence Secretary in his comparable relations on home grounds.

In November 1962, while these two entertained false

hopes of one another's plans, each evidently took for granted that the other's terms of reference were akin to his. Each erred accordingly. Despite identical titles and commensurate jurisdictions, their positions were more unlike than they realized.

Thorneycroft apparently viewed McNamara with confidence as a successful British Secretary of Defence, a man who could carry his colleagues in Cabinet. McNamara seems to have viewed Thorneycroft with hope as an effective American Secretary of Defense, a man who could enforce his will upon the Chiefs of Staff. Thorneycroft had grounds for confidence. On taking office in September he had visited the States, felt McNamara's force, and seen the President's delight in him. McNamara, in turn, had grounds for hope. That visit reportedly showed Thorneycroft to be far quicker on the uptake than his predecessor.

Thus, when Thorneycroft heard McNamara's warning about Skybolt he seems to have assumed his caller meant to cancel and would bring it off. In this he was quite right. A man who could do that surely could offer him a satisfactory substitute. In this he was quite wrong. When McNamara heard Thorneycroft say something of Polaris he seems to have assumed that his respondent would look into it and ask for it. In this he too was wrong.

I already have told you why Thorneycroft forebore to take initiative within his Ministry. He was too weakly placed to rile his Services. He was also too weakly placed in Cabinet, since the PM much preferred the status quo. Thorneycroft had just climbed back into the Cabinet by Macmillan's grace. He had no strength to muster there except what he could glean from his portfolio. These weaknesses were reciprocal.

McNamara suffered no such weaknesses. He had his Chiefs off balance. He had White House backing. And he also had the friendship of the Secretary of State, who saw things much as he did in those days. Besides, they were drawn close by shared relief in the successful outcome of the Cuban missile crisis. Within the Executive Branch, at least, McNamara never had been stronger.

It is easy to see why McNamara's hopes for Thorneycroft were disappointed, but why the disappointment in reverse? What falsified the latter's confidence in McNamara? Apparently the answer lies in a weak spot amidst his strengths which Thorneycroft seems never to have noticed: McNamara could carry his colleagues but not Rusk's subordinates, not without a fight. Presumably he could have won the fight, but not without a cost. The cost would have included inconvenience for himself, embarrassment for Rusk, and possibly a strain in their relations.

For McNamara to accompany the Skybolt cancellation with an offer of Polaris as a substitute for Britain would entangle budgetary action, where the lead was his, with diplomatic action, where the lead was Rusk's. And it would be done over the dead bodies of the Europeanists in Rusk's Department (to say nothing of his own). For reasons I already have explained, their opposition could not help but be intense. Were McNamara to accompany his cancellation with an offer, he must first take the initiative to draw that opposition from Rusk's men and to defeat it on Rusk's own terrain.

The fact that the initiative was McNamara's would

cause extra trouble. In the eyes of State Department staffers he then would be a poacher on "their" ground, a grabber of the lead which was their Secretary's, not his. What they saw would not matter in the end, provided Rusk and Kennedy saw differently. But what they said would only make it harder for those two to give the victory to McNamara. Whereas if the initiative were Thorneycroft's, not his, that difficulty scarcely could arise.

As Thorneycroft did not dare to be called traitor by his Air Force, so McNamara did not care to be called poacher in the State Department. Their risks were not commensurate. Thorneycroft might have lost his job. McNamara almost surely could have won his fight. But their side-stepping followed the same logic. Each thought he would be taken off his own hook by the other's initiative. Each lived in happy ignorance of what the other thought. Each waited for the other: Thorneycroft for McNamara's offer, McNamara for Thorneycroft's request. Each, of course, was disappointed.

Although unfortunate, their ignorance is understandable. How could McNamara grasp the inhibitions of a Thorneycroft, his presumed opposite number? McNamara's predecessors might have done so. To be cheese in a sandwich between Chief of Government and Chiefs of Staff was not for them an unfamiliar role. Possibly the McNamara of 1967 might have empathized with Thorneycroft. Not so in 1962; McNamara then had nothing comparable in his experience.

Harder still became the task of empathizing in reverse. How could Thorneycroft have grasped the inhibitions of a McNamara who to him seemed immeasurably strong? British officialdom, at least in civil service ranks, lies down when it is told to do so by its Ministers. The Foreign Office may dispute a Defence project heatedly, but let the Foreign Secretary take his colleague's side and that is usually the end of it (assuming Cabinet concurrence). Not so with us, especially not in Rusk's tenure of office, and in his case least of all on European questions. There, officials with good causes, deeply felt, would never cease to press them on him, around him, or over his head, seeking allies anywhere and everywhere in other agencies, the Services, the White House staff, the press corps, Congress, foreign embassies, or the Eastern Establishment (bulwark of bipartisanship). Had McNamara taken up his fight and won it, that would not have made an end of it. The skirmishing would have gone on, guerilla-style, for years. Apparently he was aware of that. But this remains for Englishmen among the most incomprehensible of features in our system. Thorneycroft could not have been expected to conceive that mighty McNamara, scourge of his own Services, would hesitate to tackle a few Foreign Office types.

V

This double instance of misreading by these Defense Ministers, each of the other, can be used to illustrate more than the subtleties attendant on relations among men in jobs. There also is wrapped up in it an illustration of the fourth and final category I have offered you: the category of perspectives molded by such jobs. Some transatlantic differences attendant on this category have been mentioned in my crisis summaries, most notably,

perhaps, the relative significance of the Suez Canal in
Eden's eyes and Eisenhower's. But nothing serves so well
to show what lies behind this category as the different
shades of meaning McNamara and Thorneycroft, respec-
tively, attached to national defense.

In 1962 "defense" for McNamara seems to have remained real, hence technical. Limited wars were likely
in our future. Nuclear war might be averted by deterrence of the Russians. They alone, besides ourselves, had
intercontinental nuclear capability. Deterrence turned
upon their understanding of our power to strike back
if they struck first. Their understanding turned upon
our weaponry—its character, emplacement, and control.
These turned upon technology.

For Thorneycroft, however, by 1962 "defence" apparently had come to be symbolic, hence political. Three
medium-sized H-bombs could obliterate his island. Were
these to be deterred, *our* weaponry must do it. He had
neither funds nor space to replicate our forces, and his
own made little difference independently of ours. Now
that our deterrent had been brought into the missile age,
he could not even offer us the time advantage once possessed by British bombers. Britain still was an "un-
sinkable aircraft carrier," but aircraft were no longer
indispensable to our deterrent. The RAF, even when
armed with Skybolt, would impress the Russians only
if they thought it might be used without us to strike
them. The Navy, even if provided with Polaris, would
be in the same situation. But British Ministers and
Services had no intention of striking independently. To
strike first was to invite the end of Britain. As for a
second strike, they long since had tied all their plans

to ours. Whether Skybolt or Polaris, whether aircraft or submarines, their independent nuclear deterrent was strategically irrelevant: independent it would not deter; dependent it would be superfluous. But by no means was it irrelevant politically.

In terms both of diplomacy and of internal politics, "nuclear independence" mattered much to British Ministers. So it was in Macmillan's time (and so it remains in Harold Wilson's). What mattered was the symbol. A nuclear strike force "made in Britain" and controlled there symbolized the British role in nuclear development, a comforting reminder of past greatness and a hint of future services to Europe. It also kept Great Britain in the "Nuclear Club," a haughty circle, and assured her right to claim a place in talks on the great questions of the day, not least on the defense of Europe. Further, it kept alive the "special" character of her "relationship" with us: command-control arrangements between the RAF and USAF were the most concrete links left among the many forged by World War II. Finally, Britain's nuclear force was now an issue in home politics, attacked by Labour and defended by the Tories who perceived in its defense a hold on "jingo" sentiments among the working class. This Tory vision evidently had some substance: Harold Wilson hastened to adopt Macmillan's weapons as his own, hence neutralize the issue, after Labour entered office two years later.

In the words of an official on our side, nuclear weapons had become by 1962 "the most expensive status symbols since colonies." The British were as much committed to the one as ever to the other, none more so than Thorneycroft. He had a special vision topping all the rest. He personally seems to have conceived their nuclear force as trading-stock for a deal with de Gaulle. His colleagues had not bought this vision from him at the time, but he just then was trying hard to sell it. No wonder that, as Arthur Schlesinger records, Thorney-croft and McNamara spoke in different languages when finally they met one another face to face.

Differing perspectives on the meaning of defense seem to have plagued the Suez case as well as Skybolt. In the fall of 1956, Eden seems to have believed that our prospective toleration for his cover story—separating combatants to safeguard the Suez Canal—was strengthened by our interest in the Panama Canal. If fighting were to start in its vicinity we certainly would intervene. Since we presumably knew that as well as he, we surely would not wish a precedent established against interventions on behalf of canal safety. Jewish votes aside, avoidance of the precedent should keep us acquiescent if he moved under the guise of keeping Suez safe. This reasoning had numerous deficiencies. For one, the cover story was too thin to be believable in Washington. For another, it could not be made to square with the Tripartite Declaration we immediately invoked, to Eisenhower's subsequent embarrassment. And for a third, men steeped in *our* conceptions of defense could not have been expected to imagine themselves mounting a slow-motion intervention, British-style. Far from it.

I would guess that General Eisenhower literally could not conceive of plans to safeguard Panama after a six-day sail. His turn to the UN against his allies set no precedent he could not live by; a real, not self-made, threat to "our" canal would have evoked a "real" response. Downing Street already perceived "defence" quite differently from Eisenhower's White House. If Kennedy's fiasco at the Bay of Pigs seems to belie the point, this traces rather to his inexperience than to a shift in presidential perspective. Eisenhower, it seems safe to say, would not have tolerated those plans either.

I have dug a dozen instances out of our crisis stories and have used them now to illustrate four categories equally descriptive of the British and American machines. I have done it to make plain important nuances of difference, subtle yet not slight, between those two machines. No wonder that in these same instances officials on one side misread the other side and acted in a fashion to exacerbate relations. The nuances encountered in these instances do not exhaust, by any means, the total of small shadings one discovers when one crosses the Atlantic. But these suffice, I trust, to make the point. When those officials tried to read each other right, theirs was a hard task.

Still, if we would influence an ally, inducing its machine to act as we would like, accurate perception (and commensurate response) become incumbent on American officials, with respect not only to the British but to governments where differences are greater and our knowledge less. What shall we need to make a better job of it than our men managed in the crises now before you? Or possibly does this ask more than we have reason to expect from our machine and from our intellectual resources? May it be that in these crises our men suffered not avoidable mistakes but rather limitations native to relations between governments?

These are the issues I would now address.

VI: Limits on Influence

IN THE PRECEDING chapter I have set forth a dozen instances of misperception between Washington and London. An aspect of behavior is common to all. In every instance, players on the one side failed to understand the stakes of players on the other. They failed to do so because they misread the interests which the other men pursued. They misread interests because they misunderstood, to some degree, the precise nature of the game in which the others were engaged: its positions, or its channels, or its history. Quirks of personality contributed, no doubt, but these alone cannot explain the failures I have noted. Players on both sides knew quite a lot about each other's characters. Rather, it is these combined with the peculiar settings of particular positions which account for the misreadings in my stories. Men in office are men molded by their jobs.

The question now is whether we can reasonably expect that men in such machines should have been able to do better.

I

What is the operational significance of this behavior? When a Dulles or a McNamara fails to note nuances in the British Cabinet system, when an Eden or a Macmillan fails to see a subtlety in presidential budgeting, what matters operationally to the alliance scarcely is that failure in and of itself. They are not university students; they take no courses in comparative government. They are not examined in that subject nor are their rewards and penalties determined by professors. What matters is far different: it is what they do in ignorance of what they fail to see. And what they do is guess wrong about motives on the other side: the hopes, incentives, fears, and substantive perspectives which contribute to an opposite number's stakes in his own game. Thereby they pave their way toward the disappointed expectations and the paranoid reactions characteristic of crisis behavior.

Besides, still more significant, they *act* upon their guesses, or they fail to act because of them. Thereby they forfeit chances to exert effective influence on the behavior of the other side.

As between the British and Americans, how each side acts has consequences in the other's game. What happens on the one side may affect the other's state of play, and thus the stakes of players. If one side's actions are dependent in the least upon the other side's performance, the dependence of the one becomes the other's opportunity for influence. So it was in every instance now before you. But in these circumstances influence is tantamount to action of precisely the right kind, at the right time, to make the other players reassess their interests, recompute their stakes, as they perceive them in *their* game. And if the would-be influencers guess wrong about what these other men are seeing, they will act

wrong, save by happy accident, thus forfeiting their influence upon them. So it was in all the early stages of
our crises.

Influence is inseparable from action. Influential action
turns on accurate perception. In these instances perceptions were askew. Actions were misplaced or mistimed
because motives were misconstrued. Motives were misread because of faulty understanding hidden by analogy:
the "little" differences were lost from sight.

It may appear astonishing that men so used to working
with each other, so accustomed to each other's government machines, could fail to read with accuracy one
another's motives. Between London and Washington
there had been multiple close contacts for a generation.
Since the start of World War II there had been mani-
fold joint ventures. Washingtonians of both our crises
felt at home in London, more so than in any other capital. For many of our Londoners the feeling was reversed.
Yet they did indeed misread each other. The reason is
not far to seek. Those who play at governing in London
or in Washington are playing different games by different rules. However much they mingle with each other,
every player carries in his head the rules of his own
game. On those his head depends.

Games of governance are relatively self-contained,
each in its own national machine. By this I do not mean
that any player's interests may not comprehend some
interests of another player in another national game.
Far from it, witness the RAF and USAF. Neither do I
mean that any player's personal or patriotic sentiments
may not be drawn to players in another game. Witness
Eisenhower and Kennedy in turn affectionate toward

Macmillan. Nor, finally, do I mean that actions in another game have no effect on prospects for a player in his own game. Witness Dulles weaving like a nervous cat, or Eden when the rug was pulled from under him by Humphrey. The contrary, indeed, becomes the key to influence.

Rather, self-containment means three things. First, positions are defined at home: nothing from outside the game can enter save as it impinges on those definitions. The men in both our crises only registered events abroad as these were seen to bear upon their work. Second, men grow up at home. Comprehension of their work and of their interests and each other has been shaped by a long learning on home grounds. It is necessitous learning. Other games may figure in it, but incentives for absorbing their particulars are relatively weak. Third—and this explains that weakness of incentive—men are booed and booted out at home or cheered and re-elected or promoted there. Whatever the effects on them of happenings abroad, these cannot be made manifest in their careers except at home. Self-containment, I have said, is relative. In these respects, however, it is very nearly absolute.

No wonder that despite their close acquaintance with each other, their familiarity with one another's streets, hotels, and offices, our transatlantic gamesmen often saw each other wrong. Londoners were busy watching Londoners. Washingtonians were doing likewise. Attention runs to risks. The most absorbing risks are those at closest quarters. All these men could testify to that.

It follows that the conscious exercise of influence by players in one game on actions in another is hard to do effectively. It is hard, at least, for those who have to do it. It is hard because it calls at first for an unnatural diversion of attention from necessitous concerns in their own game. And then it calls for action stemming not from those concerns but from perception of the play in quite another game. Yet such perception may belie counsels of caution in one's own game, whence one's stakes are made. This aggravates the hardship. Between London and Washington our two crises of confidence might have been softened, or averted altogether, by a number of conceivable initiatives from one side to the other. These were not forthcoming, not at least at the right time; perhaps they were not even thought of at the time. But this may be suggestive less of error than of difficulty.

II

To expose these aspects of the difficulty let me now rough out three instances in our two crises where (at least in theory) a different course of action on our side might have had significant effects upon behavior on the other side. These instances do not exhaust the might-have-beens, but they suffice, I think, to show you what is hard, and why, about endeavors to exert effective influence.

First, in the Suez crisis, Dulles could have sweetened his September effort to sell SCUA as a substitute for force had he but pledged the dollars London wanted. Presumably he need have done no more than to intimate in private—and forbear to contradict in public—our support for dollar costs of routing tankers around Africa or oil from Venezuela. Such actions would have had to wait on SCUA's formal organization; others than ourselves might then have dragged their feet. A SCUA-proclaimed "boycott" scarcely could have started before late October. Our election would be but two weeks away. Thereafter, with that problem off our backs, we might have found in Nasser's conduct reason to suggest that SCUA think again. A boycott thus cut short would not be very costly. Meanwhile, Eden would have had a showing of American co-operation he could use against his "hawks," or his "doves" could use against him, to preclude further action without our consent.

This is a subtle option, but in fact if not in reputation Dulles evidently was a subtle man. Surely this could not have been beyond his comprehension. However, almost surely, it would have exposed him to a complicated struggle with the Secretary of the Treasury, and not with Humphrey only. Worse still, that would have been a struggle on disadvantageous ground: while the Canal was functioning our shippers, let alone our Treasury, seem to have had no stomach for a boycott; neither did officials charged with resource-planning for American defense and conservation of hemisphere oil supplies. Imagine Dulles coming before Eisenhower with an "iffy"—also perhaps rather "sneaky"—proposition that cost money, lacked support, and could be justified by nothing more than notions about palace politics in Britain! I cannot imagine it. Evidently Dulles could not do so either.

Whether Dulles even toyed with it, or tried it out on colleagues and withdrew, I cannot say. There is evidence, I think, which might settle the point, but I have not had access to it. However, it is certain that he met repeatedly with Humphrey, and with other officials concerned, for lengthy conferences on Suez in the days when Londoners were pining for a boycott. Conceivably this is coincidental. I think not.

Second, a month later, in October, Dulles might have done the opposite. As British silence lengthened, while Americans read troubling intelligence reports on military preparations, Dulles might have given London a contingent version of the "ultimatum" Humphrey sent there in November. Dulles did not do so. This suggests to me a failure not of "nerve" but of imagination. And I would challenge any of you, in his circumstances, to do better. For in the first place, who could have imagined that those military preparations would be of such character as to leave ample time for blocking the canal before the allies even got there? And in the second place, who could have imagined that the military planning had no monetary counterpart to cover the contingencies attendant on this time lag? Acts of imagination suited to these tasks demand either acquaintance with the state of things in Downing Street, or at least a mind cleared for intense concentration. But Dulles, at the time, knew less of Eden's circumstances than you do now. And he had Hungary to think about, along with the American election. Besides, since mid-October Dulles had been comforted by a report through Cabot Lodge, our man at the UN, that Foreign Secretary Lloyd, while there, had promised consultation before Britain took to arms. It is not clear to me what Lloyd actually may have said, if anything, but never mind. I am told authoritatively that Dulles *thought* he had such an assurance in his pocket. Time enough for concentration when and if we ever were consulted. Tough talk in advance would violate the courteous tone of Eisenhower's previous exchange with Eden, a tone set by the President himself, so I am told. Dulles at this juncture was not inclined to contravene his President on any point, especially not prematurely.

Third, in the Skybolt crisis, Kennedy's improvisation of a fifty-fifty split in British development costs, dreamed up with David Gore en route to Nassau, was dismissed there by Macmillan out-of-hand. Skybolt as a British weapon now had no appeal to the PM. Kennedy, two days before, had sneered at it in public: "The lady had been violated . . . ." That was that. But up until the moment of that "violation," through the weeks of public crisis and the two preceding years, Macmillan had been wedded to the weapon officially and personally. This suggests that had we made our fifty-fifty offer somewhat earlier—ideally in November, well before the public crisis, but conceivably as late as McNamara's visit—it might have had profound effects on British behavior.

I do not suggest that Macmillan or Thorneycroft would have wanted the weapon on those terms. You will recall what was involved: we were to cease development on our account and to eliminate the weapon from our plans, while recognizing that the British had relied on our development. If they wished to complete the task, we would pay half the cost. They then could contract with the Douglas Aircraft Corporation—maker of the weapon—for production of however many missiles Bomber Command wanted. Financially, for Britain this was unattractive. Where previously they had contemplated no share of development cost, they now would

have to dig up half the remainder. And where previously
they had contemplated ordering their missiles as a relatively small add-on to large American orders, now production would be at their order only, with a higher unit
cost. Politically, this also was an unattractive prospect:
so much expense for something the Americans could do
without, and profiting a manufacturer in no wise under
British jurisdiction. Questions would be asked in press
and Parliament, and Cabinet: was Bomber Command
worth it? What price membership in the Nuclear Club?
For Macmillan, to say nothing of Thorneycroft, the fifty-
fifty offer almost certainly would have been unaccept-
able no matter when proposed.

However, had we made the offer earlier it would have
had one virtue they could not ignore. This might have
kept them quiet. At the very least it would have mark-
edly reduced temptations to allow a public quarrel with
us and then to press for hurried resolution. For publicly
this would have seemed a relatively generous offer on
our part, responsive to Macmillan's need, at least ostensibly, acknowledging the justice of his claim that he
had done a "deal" with Eisenhower at Camp David.
Nobody could argue that his deal committed us to make
the weapon if we found we did not need it for our
purposes. But nobody could charge us with bad faith if
we stood ready to help Britain make it for her purposes.

In Anglo-Saxon logic "half-and-half" is "fair." That
was the point of Kennedy's improvisation. Had he
grasped it earlier, there might have been no public crisis.
Macmillan probably would have had no recourse but to
turn up at Nassau, hat in hand, asking could he please
have something else, better and cheaper. If so, he

scarcely could have balked at a joint study for as long as necessary to outwait de Gaulle in Brussels.

Throughout this whole affair, the key to London's conduct was the absence of a generous gesture on our part, compensating for our own disruption of the status quo. Our gesture need not have been satisfying in substance, but to keep the Tories cool, and their right wing in check, it had to be both unimpeachable and voluntary. Its absence constituted the most galling feature of Macmillan's problem, to say nothing of Thorneycroft's. Why then was something like the fifty-fifty offer not forthcoming in November, or at latest by December 11, a full week before Nassau, when McNamara went to London? If Kennedy could think of it belatedly, then why did nobody think of it sooner?

Since it was Kennedy on whom light finally dawned, this question runs in the first instance to him. The answer seems to turn upon two points. For one, it took a crisis atmosphere together with a deadline to concentrate his mind upon Macmillan's problem. Light dawned as Kennedy was flying to their meeting. Up to then it seems that what was mainly on his mind was *his* problem, a problem set by quite another deadline: imminent submission of his January budget. He wanted Skybolt out of there. This leads directly to my other point: absent crisis and the imminence of an unpleasant meeting, any thought of bailing Britain out financially ran counter to the logic—and the politics—of budgeting. For many reasons Kennedy then wanted both to be and to appear a frugal and discriminating manager of public resources. Generosity with a price tag as large as half the cost of finishing up something we ourselves were not

to use (a quarter of a billion dollars in the next year
alone) would have appeared quixotic, at the least, to
Kennedy's "general" public, let alone the Air Force,
Congressmen, and manufacturers. It would have seemed
so, anyway, except in a context of "healing the breach"
with Britain. Thus, the light dawned on Kennedy at
just the time when what it showed him held reduced
risks for him. Perhaps he did not see it earlier because
he then could not afford it. However that may be, he
earlier is said to have shown little sympathy with tenta-
tive suggestions from the Secretary of State that we
might start to think in terms of money for the British.

Kennedy was only one man among many on our side.
What of the others? McNamara's case is clear, I think,
in what I already have told you. For a man to whom
defense was very real, Skybolt had become a bad deal
for the British, especially if built for them alone. Pounds
and dollars spent in such a cause would not be intellectually respectable, save as a last resort. McNamara
scarcely could be first to spot the virtues in a fifty-fifty
offer. But from State, supposedly, there emanates a special sensitivity to the political concerns of foreign governments. What of Rusk, the Secretary, and his subordinates?

Rusk himself apparently came closer than the rest.
Throughout November and December, he evidently
took it as a matter of course that we owed something
to the British in return for our disruption of their plans.
What that something should be he did not take time
from a busy schedule to pursue himself. But there is
little doubt that had his staffs come up with something
like the fifty-fifty scheme it would have squared with his

own train of thought. A few aides tried to do so. The staffs most centrally concerned, however, were pursuing quite another train of thought.

State's Europeanists were then intent on British entry into the EEC, and on elimination of French nuclears, lest German hunger rise, hence on the devolution of Great Britain's nuclears. Men with such perspectives—which stemmed naturally enough from their positions—found potential benefit in Skybolt cancellation: an early end to British nuclear "independence." But also, and alarmingly, they found in it the risk that we might feel obliged to compensate Macmillan with a show of special favor which actually would extend independence—as with Polaris—thereby fueling French ambition and intransigence alike. De Gaulle could threaten everything these men held dear, not least a Common Market which included Britain. Accordingly, they sought at first to postpone cancellation. This ran into a stone wall: Rusk had gone along with it. Then the most energetic of them evidently put their minds to work on stiffening their seniors against "softness" toward Britain. By all accounts they soon became the enemies of any compensation. Considering the risks they thought we ran, this is quite understandable. But it was not the frame of mind in which to seek or find a means of reconciling our risks with Macmillan's problem. The question could have been: how are we to seem generous without being "soft"? So far as I can find, these State Department staffers never posed that question to themselves, or to their colleagues at Defense, or to our Embassy in London. They were too busy leaning against softness. For this they had a reason: Rusk, McNamara, and the President were known as "anglophiles."

Besides, while State Department officers confined themselves to negative advice they stood on the strong ground of foreign policy considerations—their official business—which did not cost money and implied no opposition to the savings gained from Skybolt cancellation. Had they sought instead to counter "iffy" risks that we might ultimately hand over Polaris by a firm proposal for advance commitments of another sort, they would have stood on weak ground—interlopers in the budget process, amateurs in defense planning, intellectually disreputable. That ground would have been weak throughout November and until the aftermath of McNamara's day with Thorneycroft. By then it was too late for happy thoughts at lower levels. Public crisis put the White House center-stage.

III

I trust these three examples will bring home to you the hardship when a man inside our government confronts the need to influence men in an allied government. The difficulty does not run only from us to others. If discretion permitted, I could give you equal illustrations from the other side of Suez and of Skybolt. British efforts to exert effective influence on our behavior suffered the same hardship, went astray in comparable ways, for the same reasons.

The reasons for the hardship seem to be of two main sorts. Sometimes these show up separately, but often they are intertwined, which makes the greater trouble. I have mentioned both before. Now with these examples fresh in mind, let me restate them. First, to frame an action of one's own around the needs of players in another game calls for unnatural diversion of a busy man's attention. His attention runs first to the needs in his own game. These usually suffice to fill his mind. He cannot readily thrust them aside. For him these are necessitous concerns. Of these his stakes are made. Second, the very action that could influence the other game may threaten adverse consequences in one's own, to one's own stakes. If so, the framing of this action, much less thought about it, calls for powerful incentives overriding native caution. Incentives do arise, of course, whenever it appears that what *may* happen in another game affects one's own. But such incentives reach sufficient power only if one sees that what *will* happen elsewhere really turns on one's own doing, on an act of just this sort. Here is the worst of the hardship: such a thing is genuinely difficult to see, especially with confidence enough for risky action. So it evidently was for all the men in my examples.

These, of course, are crisis cases. They exemplify failures of friendly relations. If men on one side always found it so hard to accommodate men on the other, Washington and London would be constantly at odds. They are not. Circumstances often intervene to ease that difficult dependence upon accurate perception. Frequently, the needs of players in both games overlap or coincide. Thus, during August 1956, when Dulles needed time to keep the peace, Eden needed time to prepare for war. Or needs in one game may be matched by relative indifference in the other. If Eden's needs could have been met by friendly gestures without "teeth," Dulles was prepared, it seems, to offer any number. And sometimes one side's needs cannot be met at all except on sufferance from the other. This almost guarantees unbreakable relations while the weaker men are fully conscious of their status. Eden evidently lost that consciousness until too late, ignoring money.

Yet here, precisely, is the rub: such circumstances do not always intervene, or not effectively, to moderate dependence upon accurate perception. When they do not, a premium is placed on it, and on the confidence to follow through. The difficulty is commensurate. A crisis then impends.

Accuracy of perception and accompanying confidence are bound to be in short supply. For on the one hand, calculations are too "iffy." Responsible officials cannot lightly set aside a known and relatively certain risk in favor of an unwelcome hypothesis. And on the other hand, calculations are too "fine." Such a hypothesis can blossom into firm prediction only on the showing of events—too late—or on a show of circumstantial evidence in such detail as to discredit hopes encouraged by analogy.

Judging from our cases, men in Washington see what they need to see by the light of what they want or fear, a light they manufacture out of their own heads from the materials deposited by learning and experience. Given those materials, another government must be, at least in some degree, a "black box." The box beeps in many tones, or flashes many colors. No outsider reads its signals altogether accurately out of his experience inside a different box. But whom can he rely upon to

give a better reading than his own? Whose judgment
does he take above his own? Uncertainty casts doubt on
everybody's judgment. The responsible official, then, is
tempted to fall back upon himself. He, as we have seen,
is an imperfect instrument for gathering and sorting
fine detail on other people's motives. With an ally so
close and cousinly as Britain he may entertain illusions
on that score. Our cases tell us otherwise.

You may think it strange that the vast apparatus of
our government could not produce such circumstantial
detail on the motives of an Eden, say, as to persuade a
Dulles, or on those of a Macmillan so as to arouse a
Rusk. According to my reconstructions, these things are
not very esoteric. What motivated Downing Street, it
seems, derived from commonplaces in the bureaucratic
politics and party politics of Britain, registering on the
minds and temperaments of men long at the summit in
their country's public life. Where then was our embassy
in London? What of Britain's embassy in Washington?
The answer is that these were almost together out of
play. It is the usual answer in important dealings between these allies. It serves for both our crises.

In 1956 the British Embassy in Washington was
headed by Sir Roger Makins, until his departure from
the post early that fall. His successor, Sir Harold Caccia,
arrived there only in the first week of November. Makins
seems to have been very well informed, and close to
Dulles. Indeed, during his tenure he had shown such
sympathy for Washington that words of warning from
him in the summer months were heavily discounted, I
am told, by his superiors. He was thought to have "gone
native." So much for him. Caccia, on the other hand,

could not get in the door; arriving at the height of the
November crisis, he was made to wait six weeks before
he could present credentials. Only the Economic Minister, Lord Harcourt, kept contact with our government
in those November days. He did so through personal
friendship with Humphrey. As for our then-Ambassador
to Britain, Winthrop Aldrich, he was thought by Londoners to be of no account in Washington, hence not
a man worth telling ministerial secrets. So far as I can
find, this was an accurate appraisal. Dulles and Eisenhower, it appears, were not accustomed to rely on him
for clues to British conduct. Accordingly, as his own
published recollections show, Aldrich might as well have
been in New York as in London for all he could contribute to their sense of ministerial motives.[22]

In 1962, by contrast, Britain's man in Washington
was David Gore, now Lord Harlech, my predecessor as
Radner Lecturer. He was on terms of intimacy with the
President and deeply liked by McNamara. Also, he stood
well at home with both the PM and the Foreign Office
regulars. Gore's opposite number was David Bruce, our
Ambassador to London, whose manner, charm, and
judgment made him welcome everywhere in Whitehall
and whose elegant, terse prose made any cable he com-
posed "must" reading in Kennedy's White House.
Rarely if ever in the history of our relations have both
sides been graced, simultaneously, by Ambassadors of
comparable competence to seek, transmit, and gain a
hearing for appraisals of ministerial motives. The contrast with 1956 is striking. Yet in 1962 Whitehall and the
White House misconstrued each other's motives as before, no matter that these paragons were on the scene.

As an interpreter of London to Washington, Gore could not explain what lay behind the weeks of silence after he transmitted McNamara's warning. He was not in London and his Ministers did not pass on to him by cable what they did not tell each other or their Services. As an interpreter of Washington to London he could assess the President's good will and could obtain assurances of consultation before public cancellation. So he did. But he could not make good on these assurances; he lacked control over the scheduling of McNamara's London trip. By all accounts there was still something else that Gore could not do: he could not volunteer to London a convincing explanation of our budgetary motives. Like any other Englishman—and many Americans—he seems not to have fathomed our tactics. Their logic, probably, was too parochial for him.

What then of Bruce in London? Apparently he was as much immobilized by McNamara's warning as were Thorneycroft and the PM. Bruce seems to have been told of McNamara's phone call and also of his plan to visit Thorneycroft in London. But the telling evidently came from McNamara, not from Rusk, and Bruce, in London, had no means of knowing that "his" Secretary actually approved what was afoot. Bruce, as a diplomat of great experience—and as a former Undersecretary of State—awaited questions or instructions from the State Department. Receiving none, I gather that he prudently forebore to canvass British Ministers upon a subject McNamara shortly would take up with them.

On Massachusetts Avenue and in Grosvenor Square, an Ambassador is but one man of many. The British Embassy in Washington and ours in London teem with ministers, counselors, and secretaries of assorted rank, to say nothing of special-purpose aides from a variety of government departments. These spew vast quantities of information back and forth across the ocean. But rarely is it information of the sort to shed much light on ministerial motives. Most members of those massive staffs deal with official counterparts who often cannot comprehend what moves their Minister, still less his colleagues. Even the minority of staffers actually engaged in what our State Department terms "political" affairs— that is, diplomacy—are mostly Foreign Service Officers themselves and deal for the most part with Foreign Offices. But games of governance in Whitehall and in Washington are played routinely, day by day, outside of and around those Offices, through budgetary channels, legislative channels, and promotion channels in a party context. From these the Foreign Service types are relatively shielded. Accordingly, they often are insensitive—nobody's fault—to the very stakes most likely to move Ministers from day to day.

This is not to suggest that staffers of this sort necessarily lack competence or contacts to unearth such information if it were demanded of them. In the early 1960s I think both these embassies possessed the capability to dig it out. To this I can attest from personal observation. So far as I can judge, the case is comparable for the mid-1950s. So it probably is now. With questioning enough from home to guide their search—and to assure an interest in their product—I have little doubt that embassy officials on both sides could have discerned the details missed in 1956 and 1962. All I am suggesting is that they were ill-equipped to do so as a matter of routine, on *their* initiative. And what they might have done had they been questioned hard from home is moot. So far as I can find, in neither crisis did either side pester its embassy with questions of the sort; quite the contrary.

Perhaps had operational intelligence been part of the British apparatus in Washington, and ours in London, this appraisal might be somewhat different. Then information, "hard" or "soft," about the plots and plans of leading personalities in each machine would have flowed quite routinely to the other. How good the information and how usable and how well used are all conjectural, especially the last. But these cannot be tested, for in 1956 and 1962 it was a feature of the Anglo-American relationship that we forebore to "spy" on one another. Our external intelligence services cooperated closely *vis-a-vis* third parties but were not supposed to operate within each other's country. This convention stemmed from our wartime collaboration. So far as I know it remains in force today.

Still, it appears unlikely that a government machine which has not posed sharp questions to its embassy about details of motivation on the other side would formulate such questions for itself and pass them on if only it possessed more routine information. In a government such as ours, the barriers to formulating questions of this sort, and to transmitting them, become formidable. Temptations to analogize stand in the way, reinforced by fears of building up a case for undesired action. What embassy officials find it hard to do themselves, on their initiative, Washington officials find it hard to do for them. So, at least, it seems upon the showing of two crises.

In short, my word to you is never mind those apparatuses in situations of such close alliance. From Washington to Tokyo—an enemy become a friend, but still a stranger—embassies may play a stronger role. But in a case so cousinly as Washington and London, the problem of obtaining motivational detail is rooted at the center of these government machines. Its symptoms are the questions that responsible officials leave unasked.

IV

If failures to ask pointed questions about players in a foreign game could be ascribed to nothing more than tactics in one's own, or sheer preoccupation, then you might judge with justice that my cast of Washingtonians should have been able to do better than they did. But it seems to me that something even harder is involved than the difficulties I have catalogued so far. Therefore, suspend that judgment once again while I put this last hardship on the table.

For reasons I already have explained, tactical considerations raise high barriers against endeavoring to find out what one cannot well afford to learn. Residual uncertainty in such endeavors makes them still more suspect. And busyness makes them appear a bother. Also, "iffy" questions expose askers to discomfiture by colleagues before answers are in. Recall the mutual reticence of Thorneycroft and McNamara. Thus it becomes hard to resist comforting analogies supportive of one's own convenience, harder still to contemplate a risky action without certain need. However, in the Skybolt case, at least, men so experienced and so intelligent as those who did not probe British reactions to our warning cannot readily be pardoned on these grounds alone. For some of them the penalties would have been rather slight. At upper levels of the White House and the Pentagon and State, these hardships are reduced to inconveniences, a poor excuse.

But something else apparently was operating here, and also in the Suez case. It is a still greater difficulty than the others and different in kind. It is the hardship of transcending an accustomed frame of reference one has got inside one's head and uses to conceptualize another government. This is a matter not of governmental gamesmanship but rather of intellectual conditioning. As such, it is more our business than government's, the business of a university community.

Quite plainly, almost everyone on both sides of both crises was entrapped in early stages by conceiving of the other side as though it were a friend, and then in later stages by conceiving of the other side as possibly or surely false to friendship. One neither checks too closely on a friend's reactions nor bridles one's own anger at a friend's betrayal. The lack of questions early and the paranoia later are both related to that frame of reference, "friend." This is obvious enough. It shines through all my stories.

What is less obvious is that in every story the Americans seem to have slipped repeatedly into a mode of thought whereby they personalized their British friendship, conceiving it either as tantamount to "good old

Mac" or "Tony" or as tantamount to an intelligence of unitary sort, "clever chaps." For reasons that I think are deeply cultural, the Englishmen involved seem less prone than our people to have simplified their "friend" abroad in such a fashion, except perhaps for Eden as he contemplated Ike. However that may be, it is American behavior with which I am most concerned, and the Americans strike me as tending always to conceive relations with the other side in terms of human friendship.

On the surface this assertion may seem inconsistent with my stress in earlier chapters on the tendency of our men to perceive the other side as a projection of their interests, their concerns, and to analogize accordingly. Surely they knew, their behavior shows it, that their own side was a complex game. Projecting their concerns upon the other side seems an acknowledgement by them that it too was a game, however misperceived, and neither single-man nor solidary-group. Yet insofar as I can judge, these men thought in both modes at once, unaware of inconsistency, and actually contrived to make them mutually supportive.

When Washingtonians looked outward to assess London's constraints—hence stakes, hence ministerial motives—their frame of reference evidently tended to be realistic if parochial, akin to their experience of Washington. When they then thought about the force of these constraints they evidently tended to conceive them in a simpler frame, not as affecting complex gamesmanship but rather as impinging on a single human actor: "Tony" cautious in the face of Opposition; "clever chaps" concerting in the face of threatened change.

Thus, personalization served to compound errors rooted
in hopes nurtured by convenience and analogy.

Our minds are at the mercy of our language and our
entrenched ideas. So powerful, so nearly irresistable, at
least for us, is the conception of a "government" as
though it were a person, that even those who knew better
because they were inside one seem to have been incapa-
ble of consciously, consistently applying what they knew
when thinking of the other they knew best in all the
world, their "friend" in London.

Yet the friendship they depended on and sought to
work within was not that of two human beings. Human
friendships were part of the tangle of relationships, but
nothing like the whole. Neither was this a friendship
between single-minded centers of rational calculation.
Reasonable men engaged, of course, in calculations on
both sides, but never single mindedly on either side.
Rather, as I have said to you before, this was a friendship between government machines, the most complex
of modern institutions, with decision-making processes
resembling man's only in their self-centeredness.

Had our men consistently conceived themselves and
Londoners as players in two intricate and subtly different bargaining arenas, interacting on each other by
and through the side-effects of their internal games, then
I suspect they would have found it harder to depend
upon analogies, easier to overcome temptations of convenience, fears of risk. And almost certainly they would
have found it indispensible to formulate the questions
they appear not to have asked.

But where were they to learn such consciousness? Of
what were they to build such a conception? We all share

the same language still and think in the same modes as they. Put yourselves in their places! Do you still conceive that they should have done better? If so, why?

V

Hopefully this book can contribute something toward construction of new modes of thought about relationships between our government and its allies. But if the hope is to be realized, then the burden of construction falls on those of us who work in universities, not on the men who govern. We, not they, supposedly are specialists in thinking about ways of taking thought. And if they find it hard to think about alliance politics in terms to fit the task they face, then I can only say to you: the fault is ours, not theirs. Look at analyses of international relations. Look at diplomatic histories. Where are the frames of reference to illuminate behavior of the sort I have described? Scattered through the literature, mostly by implication. If we cannot find explicit concepts in our literature we scarcely can expect that those who have to do the work of governing will find them for themselves, suck them out of their thumbs, in the interstices of crowded days.

At Harvard now a number of my colleagues in the Kennedy School's Institute of Politics are working hard and fruitfully toward new frames of reference more sophisticated than the notions I have used throughout these chapters. What you find here, I am happy to acknowledge, is a crude first cut, an adaptation of what Graham Allison has termed "Conceptual Model III."[23] This model treats a governmental outcome as the product of internal bargaining. All I have done here is to posit that an *inter*-allied outcome is produced by interaction of such *intra*-governmental games. This is what I term alliance politics. Since I have chosen here to focus upon players at the top of Washington and London, Model III is an illuminating frame of reference.

Other frames of reference shed more light on other aspects of these games. Allison also has offered us a "Model II." This treats outcomes of governments as outputs of matured organizational units on the order of those business firms explored by Cyert and March.[24] As my illustrations will suggest, such units were at work in Suez: witness the British Army with its embarkation plans. Counterparts were equally at work in Skybolt: for example, the RAF and USAF. Rather than interactions of two bargaining arenas, these crises might be viewed as interactions of two sets of "satisficing" organizations. This approach might be no less illuminating than the other. Moreover it would highlight rather different things. Still a third approach, bearing on both these others, has been fostered by John Steinbruner: a "Model IV," which focuses attention on the fixed ideas men carry in their heads and use to screen out information.[25] This too holds promise as a frame of reference, illuminating still another set of things. And others of us shortly will begin retracing the ground explored by Columbia's distinguished former Provost, David B. Truman, to see what can be done toward bringing up to date and also turning operational his observations on political interests outside the machine. Operationally these also enter into the causation of most governmental outcomes (including inactivity). A frame of reference to illuminate the "where" and "when" and "how" holds further promise for us.

We do not pull apart these models for the sake of independent application. We have no notion that the causal factors emphasized by each are separable in real life. But having sorted these out analytically, we now are in position to begin their reassembly, asking ourselves where, against what circumstances, different combinations of those factors yield most fruitful explanations. Typology is our immediate concern: our aim becomes a single framework built of moveable parts, with indicators telling us which parts we need investigate, in what priority order, as we set about explaining given outcomes of assorted types.

Two of my colleagues are at work now trying combinations of these models on for size to see how they illuminate historical events. Other explorations of the sort will soon begin. Ernest May is reassessing the Washington Naval Conference of 1922. Samuel Williamson is studying behavior in the Viennese machine and interaction with Berlin's machine, from the Albanian crisis to the outbreak of the First World War.[26] Thereby he is looking at relations of alliance which compare most closely to the Anglo-American case.

The next step is to turn from explanation to prediction, to see what can be done with frames of reference such as these by way of posing questions that shed light upon outcomes ahead.[27] If we can take this step we shall have done our duty by the men of action. In scholarly endeavors of this sort, there are no guarantees. The academic woods are full of false trails littered by junked inquiries. Unless we try, however, there is little hope of better frameworks, better questions, in the minds of activists.

Harvard claims no monopoly; we have allies and friendly critics elsewhere, all self-propelled, not least at Columbia, for instance Warner Schilling.

Perhaps I have no reason to complain of academia. We do not seem to be more than one generation late. This country had no peacetime allies before 1945, and then, through Truman's years, its European friends remained dependent on our bounty to survive, a simplifying factor in alliance management. Peacetime alliance politics, as I have used the term, cannot be said to antedate the Korean War. Our first major experience, and misadventure, is likely to be seen historically as the EDC, the European Defense Community, where Washington's relations with the French bear interesting resemblances to aspects both of Suez and of Skybolt. When scholars start to grapple with a problem of conceptualization only a decade after their government encounters it, surely this is timely, at least as time is measured by the pace of social sciences.

Were frames of reference all we lacked to manage an alliance, and all Washington could use from academia, I now could close upon a note of moderate self-satisfaction. My subject matter lends itself, I fear, to that conclusion. But beware: Anglo-American relations are deceptive.

In the instance of Great Britain as an ally, at least during the course of our two crises, Washingtonians may well have lacked for nothing save an adequate conception of the overlapping games in which they were engaged. While in practice they had insufficient information on the British game, and on its structural detail, and on details of motivation, they did not lack for information *sources*; appropriately used—that is, to answer the right questions—these sources almost surely could have met most information needs. Both in and out of Washington the woods were full of government officials and of private citizens (journalists, professors, lawyers, bankers) with a piece, or two or three, of special knowledge about Whitehall; across the water there were quite as many Englishmen accustomed to share confidences with informed Americans.

We have no other ally of which so much can be said. Indeed, for some of our allies I probably should say the opposite: no facet of their inner politics seems to be known reliably by anyone within the reach of Washington. If so, our Washingtonians need more than frames of reference. They also need the sorts of information which could satisfy the questions better frames of reference might induce them to ask.

Consider, for example, the German Federal Republic. I cannot speak for Washington today, but I can say with confidence that a few years ago, in Washington, Bonn ranked only above Peking among the major capitals as an unknown—though not, of course, unknowable—machine. Its game of governance was understood in outline and its leading personalities in general, but the fine detail of structure, of positions, channels, stakes, and state of play was neither grasped by most of our officials nor pursued, with rare exceptions, by our scholars. In my present university, at Harvard, until very recently, we could claim two professors who were rather knowledgeable on these subjects, even though their knowledge was a by-product of other interests. In my former university, at Columbia, we could have made a comparable claim. These scarcely are impressive claims. In Cambridge it is hoped that we are starting to do better. Perhaps the hopes at Columbia are similar. However that may be, the previous situation is suggestive of American intellectual priorities: Bonn's internal politics, the inner life of that machine, has been far down our scale. No doubt there are all sorts of reasons, but the sociology of knowledge is not now my concern.

What concerns me now is the outlook for Washington, even were it armed with the right questions, endeavoring to influence this Bonn machine without the wherewithal of information to provide some answers. In the Adenauer era, and thereafter for a time, it scarcely seemed to matter whether we guessed right or wrong about what moved a German player in his own game or how our moves resonated inside his machine. Those players were so conscious of the fraility of their own machine, and so determined to hang onto us regardless, that we then possessed wide latitude for ignorance. They had no history save what we had bequeathed them in our occupation since the war, and we knew it—or thought we did—as well as they. But their machine is settling in, and their sense of dependency cannot help but be lessening with time. The German Miracle goes on and on; inducing, one supposes, increased confidence to match objective power. In coming years, if our machine attempts to influence the German course as we endeavored to shape Britain's not so long ago, Washington will need to learn of Bonn as much as it could ever have discovered about London. Whence is the word to come? On present showing, not from universities.

This is no warrant for suggesting that our intellectual priorities should be reshaped to meet the needs of government, far from it. Had there been less such reshaping in the past, we now might have more German scholars and a lesser number of somewhat redundant Sovietologists. But if our government cannot look to our universities it either must develop needed expertise itself, inside the machine, or else it must reduce its expectations of alliances.

VI

The record of the past leaves little room for hope that Washington, on its own motion, unsupported by extraordinary efforts in the universities, will nurture a sufficiency of expertise about the inner politics of governments now strange to us.

The problem here is neither men nor money. In career ranks there is talent; in administrative budgets there are funds. Both could be shaken loose and brought together for new purposes, which then could be sustained through all the time it takes to build a specialty. But none of this is practicable without unremitting interest from the top of our machine, an interest manifested in continuous concern and maintained through the life of more than one Administration. That is the problem. Not in twenty years has a Secretary of State consistently concerned himself with the administration of the Foreign Service or with its aims and measures for professional training. Not at least since Robert Lovett's time has any Secretary of Defense persistently addressed himself to the vast apparatus of professional education in and through the Military Services. As for the White House, its reactions are quite stereotyped: in the realm of training for careerists, innovations once espoused are soon lost in the shuffle; enthusiasm for reform wanes with the aging process; attention spans grow short in four-year terms; immediate concerns invariably take over.

Now we have a new Administration. Its behavior may belie these rules-of-thumb. But this is so unlikely that in prudence I discount it.

There remains the option of reducing expectations. During the past generation Washington has been remarkably self-confident about its capability to make the mechanisms of alliance serve its purposes, remarkably disposed to think that our machine could exert an effective influence on other countries through their own machines. What Washingtonians seem to have thought they needed was the will, along with money. They have not been alone in this: the thought is echoed frequently by scholars, to say nothing of the Council on Foreign Relations. But if, in fact, they also need new ways of taking thought, along with information they are unlikely to get, then possibly they would be well advised not to try harder but to attempt less.

This is a counsel of caution, not a plea for inactivity, let alone "isolation." If our capability for influence is limited, what this suggests to me is not passivity, not folded hands, but rather concentration of our effort on the work we might get done within the limits. A lot of work remains. It is work of a rather different order than we often have attempted in the past. It is, however, well within our capability.

For example, let me offer you a might-have-been from Skybolt. Macmillan, I surmise, will be assessed by history as a superb political tactician but an indifferent strategist. The underlying cause of crisis during 1962 can be traced to the tactically effective "deal" he had negotiated two years earlier with Eisenhower at Camp David. This gave Macmillan, at low cost and little inconvenience (momentarily), something on which he could rest his claims of nuclear "independence," transatlantic "interdependence." But the "something" was exceptionally complicated in conception, yet to be developed, meant for bombers with a limited life span: the Skybolt missile. Thereby he made what seems to me a classic error in high policy or politics: he pursued objectives, diplomatic and political, disguised as something else, a military posture, which was suspect in its own terms, liable to attack or ridicule or both. Yet these were the ostensible terms he had to use henceforth in justifying deeper aims.

During 1960 we could not have known what troubles our compliance was to cause Macmillan. But simple reasoning could have disclosed to us that our participation in creating such a posture and sustaining it for him invited complications between governments, opening the way toward just the sort of calculations our machine is ill-equipped to make. For at Camp David all the clues we needed were at hand, amounting very simply to the fact that Thomas Gates, our Secretary of Defense, and his civilian aides were awed by Skybolt's technical requirements, doubted our capacity to meet them, doubted furthermore that we would want it when we got it, thinking even then about Polaris and Minuteman. Despite their doubts they gave Macmillan what he wanted. Our Air Force also wanted it, which probably explains both why he asked and why they gave. Thereby they placed a time-bomb under our relations. They would have done better to search for a solution which portended simpler side-effects.

The search for simple side-effects is worthy of your notice. It becomes a quest for operationally uncomplicated means, for measures manageable with least strain on our capacity to seek and to assess the fine detail of other governments. Here is work to which we now might turn: the search for these *and the eschewing of their opposites.*

The Marshall Plan of happy memory had the requisite simplicity, despite the then unorthodoxy of its claims upon American resources. It called for us to do no more than we knew how to do through the machines of other governments which had the wherewithal to meet a shared and limited objective. Alas, it often has been cited since as precedent for ventures lacking in these saving qualities.

Our contemporary "big" bureaucracy in national security affairs, so-called, is a blunt instrument. On the record of the past it is effectively responsive to blunt challenges when gripped by a blunt policy. Its character was shaped in World War and in Cold War. Yet the era of such challenges now seems to be behind us. Blunt policy no longer serves. Subtlety, however, is a thing for which this instrument was not designed, with which I have my doubts that it can learn to cope. What remains? Simplicity.

Simplicity consists in limiting our claims on other governments to outcomes reachable by them within a wide range of internal politics, under a variety of personalities and circumstances. These are outcomes which do not depend for their achievement on precise conjunctions of particular procedures, men, and issues. Thereby accurate perception of the other side's concerns is simplified down to the point where our officials should be capable of accuracy enough for influential action. So it was with the Marshall Plan. So it was not, unfortunately, with the Camp David Agreement. In the Suez crisis our desire for an outcome that combined peace with no dollar cost invited our misreading of constraints to keep an Eden on such stony ground.

The requisite simplicity will alter from one situation to another. It apparently depends upon at least four variables in Washington's relations with an ally. First is the other government's location on a line running from tight ties toward nominal connections. Second is its location on another line running from familiarity toward strangeness. These two are not the same; compare London with Bonn. Third is our command and use of needed expertise (also, of course, its quality). Fourth is our freedom of choice, whether constrained by an outside event or open to the play of interests, or somewhere between.[28]

In the Skybolt case we dealt with an ally at once so strongly linked and so familiar that we felt no need for experts and relied instead on hunches. We did so the more readily because we were constrained by no outside events. During the crucial middle months of Suez—after Nasser's seizure but before Hungary—the situation was about the same. We pledged ourselves to outcomes on the British side. By hindsight their achievement was too complicated for our comfort. But that pinch might have been eased by a determined use of expert knowledge well within our reach.

Other situations seem to offer far less leeway. I have cited Bonn to you as one example of an ally where our capability for complicated dealings could be limited. But Bonn seems relatively easy as compared with, say Bangkok. There we have strong ties accompanied by strangeness, with our choices subject to constraints of war. The combination cries aloud for expertise. Without it we are rash to hitch our star to *any* outcome stemming from the actions of those strangers. Yet in common with the rest of Southeast Asia, Thailand is a country few Americans know well enough to claim even a superficial grasp, whether of culture, or of history, or politics. Still, Bangkok seems simplicity itself compared with Saigon.

On November 15, 1963, I sent to President Kennedy a long postmortem on the Skybolt crisis, prepared at his request. It was, of course, a confidential paper for his purposes and dealt with many things at many levels of both governments besides those cited in these public chapters. Even so, some observations and reactions struck me at the time as still more confidential, not for mention even in a privileged paper. So I sent along a cover-note, explaining that there were some things I had not put on paper and preferred to give him orally. He read the report on November 17. He then sent word that he would see me after he returned from Texas. Of course

I did not see him. But before November 22 I had spent some time revolving in my mind, as one does with a President, what I should say and how. One of the things I toyed with lay outside of my assignment, to say nothing of my field for observation: I considered asking whether, in the light of our machine's performance on a British problem, he conceived that it could cope with South Vietnam's. Had I seen him I might well have lacked the time to ask, or the presumptuousness. But it was a good question, better than I knew. It haunts me still.

Notes

1. United States Senate Subcommittee on National Security and International Operations, 89th Congress, 1st Session, *Hearings,* Part 3, June 29, 1965.
2. Among the many books on Suez I have found two especially useful for present purposes. These are Hugh Thomas, *The Suez Affair* (London: Weidenfeld 1966), and Herman Finer, *Dulles Over Suez* (Chicago: Quadrangle, 1964). Thomas concentrates on the English side of the story, emphasizing interpersonal relations in Whitehall. Within these limits his account is perceptive, sensitive, and —so far as I can check from my own interviewing—very accurate. Thomas writes at two levels, one for the general reader and the other for insiders: the best of his book is found between the lines and in footnotes. Finer is more problematical. His book is much more detailed, and its coverage extends to Washington as well as Whitehall. As an annotated chronology, it is indispensable for Suez researchers. But Finer's judgment is so shaped by passion against Dulles that his characterization of events and attribution of motives are untrustworthy. Even his characterization of documents (he obviously was shown many) need be treated with some reserve.

Military aspects of the Suez campaign are underplayed in both these books. Readers interested in "Musketeer" will find an illuminating account in A. J. Barker, *Suez: The Seven Day War* (London: Faber, 1964).

As for parliamentary, press, and public attitudes in Britain, the most comprehensive work is Leon Epstein's *British Politics in the Suez Crisis* (Urbana: University of Illinois Press, 1964).

Memoirs of participants are unrevealing of detail but rather interesting in their show of retrospective attitudes. See, for example, Anthony Eden, *Full Circle* (London: Cassell, 1960) and Dwight D. Eisenhower, *Waging Peace* (New York: Doubleday, 1965). Another memoir filled with details of self-serving sort is Anthony Nutting's *No End of a Lesson* (London: Constable, 1967). His testimony, even the conversations he reports, appears to me almost irrelevant for present purposes.

3. The most comprehensive published account of the Skybolt crisis and its origins on both sides of the Atlantic is Henry Brandon's feature story in the London *Sunday Times* (December 9, 1963). It is a superb piece of journalism. Arthur Schlesinger's briefer treatment in *A Thousand Days* (Boston: Houghton Mifflin, 1965), pp. 544–66, is interesting chiefly for its characterizations of key conferences in London and at Nassau. Another interesting work, which seems to have drawn heavily on French and State Department sources, is Robert Klieman's *Atlantic Crisis* (New York: Norton, 1964). Klieman treats Skybolt in the context of Kennedy's "grand design" and Britain's bid for Common Market membership. In my view, Klieman's context and his sources have misled him in certain respects, but his account is well worth reading. Theodore Sorenson's *Kennedy* (New York: Harper, 1965), makes only fleeting reference to the Skybolt affair, pp. 564–76; it is, however, a reliable characterization.

4. Various writers ascribe the cooling of British and American interest in financing Egypt's Aswan project to personal pique on Eden's part and Dulles's because they felt affronted by some action in particular on Nasser's part. Thus

Anthony Nutting, *No End of a Lesson,* pp. 28–35, emphasizes Eden's anger when the King of Jordan abruptly dismissed Glubb Pasha in March 1956, allegedly at Cairo's instigation. Thus Herman Finer, *Dulles Over Suez,* pp. 42–43, emphasizes Dulles's anger two months later when Cairo offered diplomatic recognition to Peking. I doubt such personalized particulars as explanations for the shift on Aswan, although these may have played a minor role. Rather, I would judge that for both men—and for Eisenhower—the affront that mattered was the obvious one, far more substantial: Nasser's arms deal with the Czechs. In its aftermath, these men were persuaded by their Arabists that Nasser's hopes for the high dam at Aswan, an exceptionally large and complex undertaking, might provide the leverage to turn him around. Reportedly, neither Eden nor Dulles had much faith in this approach when they agreed to try it. Six months later, neither saw results to falsify his pessimism. Meanwhile, our Senate, disinclined in an election year to favor those who took assistance from the East, was working up to action barring any aid for Egypt, let alone exceptional assistance, if Aswan were not dropped from our agenda. Those I have been able to consult who then were in close touch with Eden or with Dulles are agreed upon this explanation for their shift of view on Aswan. I accept it. It is less dramatic than a "devil theory," which I take to be part of its strength.

5. Finer, *Dulles Over Suez,* pp. 51–52, and many other commentators claim that Dulles acted impulsively, in anger, at the close of his meeting with Egypt's Ambassador, and also that he did so without notice either to the White House or the British. I am entirely confident that none of this is so. Actually, as his calendar discloses, Dulles met with Eisenhower first, then phoned the British Ambassador, and then saw Nasser's envoy. I am told on excellent authority that Eisenhower had approved what Dulles was to say to the Egyptian, and that he said it, word for word, at the start

of their conversation. Meanwhile, he also had informed the British of it, again word for word, although London did not hear, of course, until after the fact.

6. See especially the President's letters to the Prime Minister of July 31 and September 8, 1956. These state the American logic most completely, although with more courtesy than clarity. The letter of September 8 is summarized in Finer, *Dulles Over Suez,* pp. 216–17. The summary gives rather less than the full flavor of the argument adduced in Eisenhower's text.

7. Robert Menzies, the Australian Prime Minister, chaired the delegation which presented the original eighteen-power plan to Nasser in Cairo. As the Menzies party arrived in Egypt to begin its mission, they heard news of a remark by Eisenhower at a press conference, that "the United States would go to every length to secure a peaceful settlement" (Thomas, *The Suez Affair,* p. 72). Thomas reports that Menzies was angered, feeling that Eisenhower "had pulled the rug clean out from under his feet." I am told, in addition, that Menzies conveyed his feelings to Eden, adding to the Prime Minister's own sense of outrage.

8. Informants in whom I have confidence, who have seen all the relevant American files which I have not, assert that Henry Cabot Lodge, our Ambassador to the UN, had informed Dulles of a private assurance to this effect from Selwyn Lloyd. Further, they assert that Dulles personally relied on this. I have no confirmation from my British sources, which may mean much or nothing.

9. It does not surprise me that what seems to have dominated White House thinking at this time was a fear of Soviet miscalculation. We have another instance of the same type in the 1962 Cuban missile crisis: what decided President Kennedy on a blockade rather than an air strike or invasion seems to have been his fear of forcing Khrushchev into a position from which he could not back down. (See Robert

F. Kennedy, *Thirteen Days: A Memoir of the Cuban Missile Crisis,* New York: Norton, 1969). In 1956, as in 1962, this particular fear seems not to have been widely shared by Pentagon or State officialdom.

10. From the start Gates is said to have supported Skybolt grudgingly. His civilian technical advisers were as dubious about its guidance system in 1959 as McNamara's were in 1962 (which scarcely is surprising since one of them, John Rubel, carried over). Gates seems to have accepted Skybolt initially because he understood the British wanted it. But Watkinson is said to have asked for it because he understood our Air Force wanted it. In Eisenhower's years the Air Force had the largest share of our defense budget and seemed in British eyes to dominate the Pentagon. Watkinson was determined to stay in step with SAC. Thus, Skybolt's birth in Anglo-American agreement seems to parallel its death in disagreement, with USAF-RAF relations forcing reticence upon essentially like-minded Defense Ministers.

11. In the event, while other Service Chiefs did join the Air Force in supporting Skybolt, the new JCS Chairman, General Maxwell Taylor, is said to have accepted McNamara's logic. Presumably he could afford to do so, being new in office and encumbered by no prior record on the matter in collegial relations with his present associates.

12. For details on London press reactions and their sources, which elevated this affair into a public crisis, see the forthcoming doctoral dissertation by Leon V. Sigal, "Reporters and Officials," now in preparation at Harvard University.

13. Schlesinger, *A Thousand Days,* p. 861.

14. For details on American press coverage see Sigal, "Reports and Officials."

15. Brandon, *Sunday Times.*

16. The British delegation did not share with their American confreres the details of that de Gaulle-Macmillan

conversation. So far as I can find, neither did Macmillan share them with his friend the President. Reportedly, the reason for this reticence was fear of press leaks from our side. De Gaulle could have made more of these as an excuse to scuttle EEC negotiations than actually he did make of the Nassau Conference. Or so the British evidently feared.

17. The full historical impact of the Suez crisis on Great Britain encompasses far more than political and military particulars, more even than the painful psychological effects attendant on displaying British feebleness as a world power. Still other psychological effects, less obvious but perhaps more significant, are dramatized in P. M. Newby's latest novel, *Something to Answer For* (London: Faber, 1968). These are mass psychological phenomena, involving others than the elite, and the young more than the old; these run to what in the United States we currently term "credibility" of government, including its moral worth. By no stretch of the imagination could the Skybolt crisis claim a comparable place in history.

18. One can say as much of the "external" relations between such great American departments as Defense and State, or Labor and Welfare, to say nothing of Agriculture and Interior, where "friendship" is a function of enforced confederation policed, somewhat, by presidential agencies. Relatively speaking, however, "friendship" may well be less blinding, less encouraging of hopeful misperceptions, between "allies" like these than in the case of Washington and London. Some American departments habitually regard each other much more on the model of Washington and Moscow: uncertain how to see and weigh internal differences but rendered conscious of them by habitual cross-purposes.

19. See my *Presidential Power* (New York: Wiley, 1960), Ch. 6. See also Emmett Hughes, *The Ordeal of Power* (New York: Atheneum, 1962), pp. 205-208.

20. This note, dated October 9, 1956, covers the text of a speech delivered October 8. From unclassified correspondence in the Dulles Papers at Princeton University.

21. As one concrete example, Dulles's calendars show him to have conferred with the President before every move he made either publicly or toward the British during the whole course of the Suez affair up to the moment of his hospitalization. The memories of White House and State Department associates also are indicative. In interviewing both for this book and for *Presidential Power*, I found general agreement on Dulles's punctiliousness in dealing with Eisenhower. This was generally taken to reflect the Secretary's deep concern for gaining and keeping the President's confidence. It often is said that he leaned over backwards to avoid Dean Acheson's troubles with Congress. He evidently was no less intent on avoiding James Byrnes's troubles with Truman.

22. Aldrich subsequently wrote an article for *Foreign Affairs* (Winthrop W. Aldrich, "The Suez Crisis: A Footnote to History," *Foreign Affairs,* Vol. 45, No. 33, April 1967) to tell "the story of what happened as seen from the American Embassy in London." His version reveals, I think, how marginal was his involvement in and perception of the matter. One gains this impression not only by his own admission ("I was never asked my opinion on matters of policy," he remembers, "except when Dulles was in London or I accompanied Eden to Washington") but also in light of what is known from other sources. Aldrich asserts, for example, that "when the British thought it necessary as a result of the Suez operations to strengthen their position in dollar reserves, the United States Government cooperated fully and gladly in making available the full amount which could be drawn by the British from the International Monetary Fund."

23. See Graham T. Allison, "Conceptual Models and the Cuban Missile Crisis," *The American Political Science Re-*

view, Vol. LXIII, No. 3, September 1969, pp. 689–718. See also Allison's forthcoming book, *Bureaucracy and Policy*, of which this article is an all-too-brief summary. Allison's work is central to collegial efforts underway at Harvard in what is titled, somewhat ponderously, the Research Seminar on Bureaucracy, Politics, and Policy (colloquially, the "May Group," after its chairman, Professor Ernest R. May). Brief characterization of these efforts is offered in my text. This Research Seminar has grown out of a Faculty Study Group dating from 1966, the first of its kind to be established in the Kennedy School's then newly-founded Institute of Politics. Allison was the Study Group's first Rapporteur. His book derives in part from its discussions and in part has been the spur that drove them on.

24. The reference is to Richard M. Cyert and James G. March, *A Behavioral Theory of the Firm* (Englewood Cliffs, N.J.: Prentice-Hall, 1963). See especially Ch. 6.

25. John Steinbruner's forthcoming book, which will carry on where Allison leaves off, is an outgrowth of his doctoral dissertation for the Massachusetts Institute of Technology, "The Mind and the Milieu of Policy-Makers: A Case Study of the MLF," 1968.

26. Samuel Williamson's first book, *Politics of Grand Strategy: Britain and France Prepare for War, 1904–1914* (Cambridge, Mass.: Harvard University Press, 1969), was well under way before he began to pool his efforts with those of Allison, May, Steinbruner, my own, and others in our Research Seminar. But it foreshadows much of what we are now doing in that Seminar and has affected my own thinking in this book.

27. What modest hopes I have are fueled in part by an attempt of mine in 1964 to make predictive use of the conceptual model employed in this book. As an academic exercise, to test predictive capabilities, I undertook in June of 1964 to survey the London scene and then to put on

paper my anticipation of a Labour Government's reactions to the multilateral force (MLF), should Labour win the forthcoming General Election (which ensued in October). I volunteered a copy of this paper to friends in Washington. Xerox machines being what they are, some four years later it was published, to my personal embarrassment, by magazines in London and New York. How it reached them I am unaware, nor does it matter. Publication caused some dinner-table talk in London. English friends inform me that a Cabinet Minister who had been a subject of discussion in the paper rated it in retrospect as "eighty percent accurate; twenty percent less so." Others, I gather, rate the accuracy a bit higher. I am glad to settle for eighty percent, which I regard as quite sufficiently encouraging. For anyone who cares, the text of this predictive exercise (typographical errors and all) is to be found in the *New York Review of Books,* December 5, 1968, pp. 37–46; also in the *New Left Review,* September-October 1968, pp. 11–21.

28. A typology deriving from these variables has been suggested to me in a free-hand diagram drawn by my Harvard colleague Edwin O. Reischauer, former American Ambassador to Japan. I have preserved this carefully. It is a most suggestive document for which I owe him thanks.

Index

Accountability, political, 81 ff.
Acheson, Dean [U.S. Secretary of State, 1949–1953], 158*n*21
Aldrich, Winthrop W. [U.S. Ambassador to U.K., 1953–1957], 131, 158*n*22
Algeria, 14–15, 35
Alliance politics, *see* Politics, alliance
Allison, Graham, xii, 139–40, 158–59*n*23, 159*n*26
American Political Science Review, 158–59*n*23
Amery, Julian [U.K. Secretary for Air, 1960–1962; Minister of Aviation, 1962–1964], 38
Analogy, reasoning by, 45, 67 ff., 81, 83 ff., 89, 107, 137 ff.
Aswan Dam, 10–11, 105, 153–54*n*4
Atlantic Crisis, 153*n*3
Atomic Energy Act, 31

Bagehot, Walter, 82
Baldwin, Stanley [U.K. Prime Minister, 1923, 1924–1929, 1934–1937], 12
Barker, A. J., 152*n*2
Behavior, crisis pattern of, *see* Expectations, disappointed; Perceptions, muddled; Reactions, paranoid; Reticence
Behavioral Theory of the Firm, A, 159*n*24
Ben-Gurion, David [Prime Minister of Israel, 1949–1953, 1955–1963], 85

Brandon, Henry, 52–53, 153*n*3, 156*n*15
British Politics in the Suez Crisis, 153*n*2
Bruce, David K. E. [U.S. Ambassador to U.K., 1961–1969], 132
Bundy, McGeorge [Special Assistant to the President, 1961–1966], 43
Bureaucracy and Policy, 159*n*23
Bureaucratic politics, *see* Politics, bureaucratic
Butler, Richard A. [Leader of the House of Commons, 1955–1961], 29, 101–103
Byrnes, James F. [U.S. Secretary of State, 1945–1947], 104, 158-*n*21

Caccia, Sir Harold [U.K. Ambassador to U.S., 1956–1961], 130–31
Camp David, 32–36, 89, 147
Cape of Good Hope, 18–19, 48, 119
Chamberlain, Neville [U.K. Prime Minister, 1937–1940], 102
Channel, action, 76, 80, 88 ff., 91 ff., 96 ff., 108–109, 124–25
China, 43, 154*n*4
Churchill, Sir Winston, 8–9, 68
Clifford, Clark [Special Counsel to the President, 1946–1950], 84
Columbia University, x, xi, 142
Communication, stifled, *see* Reticence
Communists, 13
"Conceptual Models and the